BUILDING YOUR OWN ECONOMY
#BYOE

BUILDING YOUR OWN ECONOMY

Your guide to true INDEPENDENCE and FREEDOM

DAVID A. PEREZ

Copyright ©David A. Perez
All rights reserved

ISBN: 979-8-53627-199-5 (Paperback)

I dedicate this book to my parents, Jesus & Elvira Perez.
You set the foundation for all that I am today.
Thank you for believing in me!

TABLE OF CONTENTS

Introduction. 9

Chapter 1: Defining Economies. 30

Chapter 2: The Components that Build Your Economy . . 39

Chapter 3: A Foundation of Freedom 51

Chapter 4: Defining your Mindset. 60

Chapter 5: Building Your Rules 73

Chapter 6: Building Your Health 90

Chapter 7: Building Your Wealth 99

Chapter 8: Building Your Legacy 108

Chapter 9: We Can't Build Anything Without Faith 116

Chapter 10: We're Better together (BONUS) 122

Conclusion: This isn't the end, it's only the beginning!. . . 129

Acknowledgements 133

BUILDING YOUR OWN ECONOMY

THE CHAPTER BEFORE WE BEGIN

INTRODUCTION

———

What if I told you that you hold the power to build and control your own economy? Would you believe me? Then, what if I told you that creating your own economy is the only way to live? It may sound crazy, but it's possible!

If you're about to read this book, there are a few things you should know. This book is going to be something you've never heard before. I will share with you ideas that have taken my entire life to clarify and put down on paper. You will be challenged to think differently. In fact, I would even say you'll feel threatened. Not by me but by your inner desires to stay the same. They will tell you to put the book down. I'm here to tell you, YOU NEED TO KEEP READING!

I've been an avid book reader for the last eight years. I've committed to learning and gaining information from as many sources as possible so I can be better equipped to take on the world for my business, and most importantly, my life. This book is an accumulation of the ideas and concepts I've learned from all those different sources. I hope that through this, you'll come to the conclusion that building an economy is right for you.

This book will give you a solid, fundamental, easy-to-understand framework that will put you in the driver's seat on the road to freedom in life.

LET'S BEGIN.

For many years of my life, I searched for mentors, coaches, professionals, and others who could help me get to the next level in my career, my life, my relationships, but most importantly, my future. As I researched and learned so much from these wonderful people, I began to formulate my own methods. This book combines all the teachings, readings, and experiences (good and bad) I have accumulated over the years, and puts it together in a way that's good and easy to understand. Most importantly, it's presented in a way that anyone who reads this book can benefit from.

This book is for anyone who wants to make a change in their life. It's for people who want to stop being dependent on the world. It's for people who want to live life on their own terms – being able to do what they want, when they want, with whom they want, and at any time they want. This is a life I wish for you, your family, and your friends. A life of freedom.

In our lives, we are constantly challenged by the power of outside forces. I call those forces… the outer economies. In simple terms, economies are the things outside our control that impact our quality of life. People go through life getting barraged by outside forces such as natural disasters, the fluctuation of the stock market, global pandemics, or even just a boss's bad attitude. The economy is all around us in everything we do, but I don't believe we were put here to have our lives shaped by what's going on outside us or outside our businesses, especially when the only control we have is over ourselves.

It is my belief that our lives are a gift from God, and how we live our lives is our gift back to God. The creation of a personal economy is part of that. Your economy is going to drive you to be able to do great things in the world. If you're reading this book today, it's because you know there's something greater for you and you're ready to take charge of your economy to attain the freedom and success you were destined for. **This means you're tired of being a victim to whatever happens in the world, and you've made a conscious and clear decision to draw a line in the sand. This means you will no longer allow the world to influence how you live your life. You will now influence the world you create by controlling your own economy.**

THE IMPORTANCE OF INDEPENDENCE

I was born on November 5, 1983, to a young, single mother who had yet to figure out life. I know it was an accident and an unplanned event in her life. Having me must have been tough. I'm sure she had some aspirations of raising me and starting a family with the man who conceived me but that didn't come to pass. The day I was born, my biological father denied me and abandoned my mother. If that wasn't hard enough on her, she was holding a newborn baby boy who was very different. You see, I looked nothing like most Hispanic babies. I looked so different that maybe my biological father heard I didn't look normal and made a decision I wasn't his child. The difference between me and most Hispanic babies was my extreme paleness. I was so pale the doctors didn't know what was wrong with me. I had life-threatening medical complications at birth, but it was very apparent I was also different in appearance. The doctors researched what was different about me and came to the conclusion that I was special. They called me special because they diagnosed me with a condition so rare that only 1 in 20,000 babies are born with it. They diagnosed me with Albinism. The more common name used by many is Albino, a term I hate, by the way.

The most notable factor that impacts people with Albinism, is a lack of pigment in their skin. Pigment is the color that makes up a person's skin tone. Not only does it affect color but it also protects skin from the harmful rays of the sun. Very simply put, I'm EXTREMELY white. Albinism impacts vision and most people with Albinism have low vision or are legally blind. Albinism causes sensitivity to bright lights and makes it difficult for us to open our eyes when exposed to bright lights or even the sun.

The day my mother took me home the doctors had already given her some advice. They said, "Keep him out of the sun and protect him. He will be a special needs child."

Once my mother left the hospital she was off to raise me on her own. A child raising a child. Add to that a special needs child. This must have been tough. I know she tried her best to take care of me and raise me as best she could. It was probably the toughest job she could have taken on. My grandparents saw her struggles and asked if they could care for me until she could get to a better place in life. She agreed, and they took me in. She wasn't abandoning me, but rather she was protecting me. I believe she knew with them I would have a better life. I truly thank her for this. My grandparents took me in when I was just one year old and raised me as if I was their child. Throughout this book, I will refer to them as my parents.

Growing up, I was treated as a special-ed kid. I was sheltered and coddled because everyone thought I needed to be protected. I rode the little bus to school, which started at the age of 3. It's common for special needs kids to start school earlier than most. I was always given extra attention. I was prevented from going outside so I wouldn't get burned. I always smelled like sunscreen, and they made me wear HUGE sunglasses that were bigger than my head. My parents worked hard to protect me from things they thought were bad for me which was almost everything! They believed my vision was too poor for me to be left alone. They believed exposure to the sun was going to lead to cancer. They believed I was going to have to be watched all the time.

Not only was I treated as a special kid, but I was also being sold the idea that I was going to be a dependent all my life.

My parents always took the advice of the many doctors I saw and listened to people they thought were experts. Little did they know, all this deeply affected my young mind. It was truly stripping away my freedom.

As you might imagine, being a child with zero color living in an area where 99% of the population is Hispanic, was very difficult as well. I was picked on a lot. Other kids called me names like "Casper," "Snowball," and "Guero," which is Spanish for "white boy." It felt as if the world had it in for me. The doctors made me feel helpless and the world thought I was a joke.

Although this was going on, I didn't realize there was so much going against me. I just thought it was how the world was. My parents believed most of the things those doctors said about me because they didn't know things could be any different. They never put me in a position to fail. They always wanted to make sure I was safe, secure and protected. They did their best with the information they had.

Growing up, I witnessed my parents working really hard to put food on the table and take care of me. My aunt, uncle, and mother were around a lot as well and my parents had to take care of them too. I will refer to them as my brother and sisters.

My parents didn't have much, but what they did have they earned with their hard work. There was never extra money for things like vacations or eating out. All their hard work was used to pay for us to live, eat, and put a little money in savings. The little trips we did take were to visit my great-grandmother who lived in Corpus Christi, TX, a city about two and a half hours away from our home. I can't remember ever eating out at a restaurant when I was growing up. Not once. It wasn't because we were dirt poor, it was because my parents had a different mindset about money. They felt they needed to protect and save everything they could for our future, so they spent very little money on anything they considered extra. Though they didn't make much money, they always made sure they saved money. My family didn't ask for handouts, even though we were probably eligible. We were poor, but we never received government assistance and they truly believed it was their job to support themselves and our family.

I look back on all those years in awe. It was incredible the way they worked so hard and gave so much. I recall the time when our water heater broke. This was a very crappy experience! It was late fall and during this time of year, it was cold outside. I thought for sure they would go down to Sears and buy a new one. But no, they didn't do it! They decided to hold off on buying one. I know for a fact they had enough money saved to buy a new one, but they didn't want to touch their savings. Their solution was to work a little harder over the next two weeks so they could buy a new one. During the time without a water heater, my mother boiled water for each of us to bathe with. It was so crazy, having to go to the kitchen to get a pot of hot water so you could bathe. Although this may sound horrible to most, I'm so thankful for that experience. That was one of my first lessons on sacrifice and commitment. As many lessons are, I can now see how this impacted me. But I didn't see it back then.

BEING A BURDEN

Early on, I picked up on the fact that my parents wanted to protect me. They wanted to ensure that they, or someone, was going to be there to take care of me. The doctors told them I was going to be special, and they believed it. All my life they planned to take care of me.

Around 16-years-old, I experienced one of the first "aha" moments in my life.

I came home from school one day and saw my parents having a serious conversation with two gentlemen wearing suits and ties. This was very unusual because we rarely had visitors, much less those in suits. They introduced me to the two men and asked me to sit down. The gentlemen were from a life insurance company and my parents said they needed to ask me a few questions. They asked some basic questions and some more thorough questions about my condition. My parents must have told them I was special. After I answered all their questions, they packed up their paperwork and left. At the time, I thought this was unusual but I didn't think much of it.

The men came back a few weeks later with a life insurance policy for me. I didn't understand why I needed life insurance at such a young age. I thought life insurance was for people who were preparing to die. I put some serious thought into this at the time because it was very scary, to say the least. I later realized my parents took out a life insurance policy because they anticipated me being a dependent of theirs forever. If something happened to them, they wanted to make sure someone else would take care of me. This was a shock to me because I never, for a moment felt like I wasn't capable of taking care of myself. This was a big turning point for me. It made me rethink how I wanted to live my life. I hated the feeling of knowing someone would have to take care of me.

After that, I started thinking of myself as a burden to my parents and worried I would always be a burden to someone. Although I didn't protest about the life insurance policy at the time, that horrible feeling of being a burden stuck with me.

WHEN MY FREEDOM WAS STRIPPED AWAY

In my mid-teens, I asked my parents to buy me a car. They told me I was crazy that I could never own a car. You see, as a child, my parents were told that I had a horrible vision and I would never be able to do some of the most basic things for myself. One of those things was driving a car. So when I asked for a car, they told me no because they thought it was impossible for me to drive. I asked if we could go visit the doctor to see if anything had changed with my vision. Of course, the doctor didn't test my eyes or do any research, he just simply told me, "You can't drive." This was so devastating to me. It wasn't because I wanted to look cool, it was about the freedom that came from being able to go somewhere on my own. The freedom of exploring. It was part of my manhood. How would I ever pick up a girl for a date if I couldn't drive a car? I remember crying all the way home from that visit to the doctor. It truly made me feel as if I would be a dependent forever, and it validated what everyone had been saying all my life.

SEEKING MY INDEPENDENCE

When I graduated high school, I was at a crossroads in my life. I had a decision to make. Should I fulfill the doctor's diagnosis and stay safe and secure with my parents, or should I make a change in my life?

I decided to give it a go and I convinced myself to go to college. I enrolled in a local community college not far from my house. This gave me some freedom, but it also ensured that I could fall back into being safe if anything didn't work out. I failed every class I registered for that year. It wasn't because I was stupid, it was because I wasn't committed. I was still trying to figure out if I was special or not. I became a heavy drinker and smoker that year. Both lead me to poor health and a dependence on my parents for money.

After failing my first year in college, I decided to give it another shot. I went to register for classes and the school told me I couldn't enroll. I had been placed on academic suspension for my poor grades, and, if I wanted to return, I had to make some large payments to get back in good standing. Although I wanted to try, I knew I couldn't afford it. I decided to look for other options, which led to another school. This was a university and not a college, but it was much further away from my home. This scared me. I didn't have a car, I didn't have a driver's license, I didn't have money and I didn't know anyone going there. This all weighed heavily on my mind. I talked to my parents and told them I wanted to enroll there, but I would have to move to the dorms. They told me they would support me and help me in any way they could.

In my second year of college, I was living on campus about an hour away from my house. This was my first taste of independence. I was still financially dependent on my parents, and I felt like this was my opportunity to figure life out. Although I told myself this was the right move, I still didn't fully commit. Every weekend, my parents would pick me up so I could go spend time at home. They would feed me and take care of me. This felt good at the time. On my weekend visits home, I would hang out with my friends from high school. Many of them were trying to figure out life just like me. I continued this lifestyle for two years.

As I entered my 20s, I didn't have a plan for life. I knew that safety and security awaited me in staying with my parents, but I was fighting to find my independence. On one of my weekend visits home, I went to a party with a few buddies, and my friend Richard asked me what I wanted to do with my life. He could see I was lost. I confided in him the fact that I was very confused and lost. He probed and asked, "What interests you?" I thought for a minute, and "real estate" is what came out. He then asked, "What about real estate?" I replied, "Well, I want to own some property." He said. "Okay, how do you plan on doing that?" I said, "I have no clue. I don't have any money, and I don't have a job. I depend on my parents, and they don't have much money either." He then said, "Well, why don't you get into real estate, but as an agent?"

That thought had never crossed my mind. Something clicked, and the concept of selling real estate was another "aha" moment. That night, I got home and did some research online. I found a school that taught the required courses I needed, and that's where my journey to independence began.

It took me about a year, but I got my real estate license and that was the first encounter I had with the concept of owning my own economy. Once I got my license, I had confidence I'd never felt before. Accomplishing something I had set as a goal felt so amazing to me. Many people may not ever understand this feeling, but having lived the life I had, I was so proud. I turned my attention to my next goal, driving! I knew those doctors were wrong when I was a teen. They were basing their opinions on case studies and outdated information. I knew I could drive. I knew my vision was good enough and I wasn't going to accept their opinion anymore. I decided to challenge the doctor who had told me

I couldn't drive, by asking him to refer me to a different doctor who specializes in Albinism. Once I met this new doctor, I knew I was in good hands. I finally found someone who wasn't just calling me special. The doctor examined me thoroughly and ran a lot of tests. He told me the previous doctor was wrong, and there was no reason I shouldn't be able to drive. Oh My God! That was a HUGE win for me. I solidified all I had believed within me for so many years. I had allowed those damn doctors to tell me what they wanted, and I never once stood up for myself. When I finally did, look what happened!

Finally, it was time to get a car! Many of my friends and many teens go through the experience of getting their first car, but I never had that until I was almost 21-years-old. Not only was I going to gain more independence than I had ever experienced before, but I was also about to start my career as a real estate agent. That same month, I took out a student loan and used that money to buy my first car! It was a 1994 Nissan Sentra. It wasn't much, but it represented freedom to me.

BACK TO BEING DEPENDENT

In 2006, I got my real estate license, and the market was flourishing. There was so much going on in the market and it meant tons of opportunities for me. I started to make what I called "good money" at the time, but I knew that I wasn't giving my best. It took about a year-and-a-half before I started taking real estate seriously and, only then did I start to see freedom in my sights. It was all coming together.

Then, before I could really give it my all, something happened. All of a sudden, it was as if I was playing a game of musical chairs and the music stopped. I heard the music stop and looked around for a seat, but there was none. The real estate market crashed and our national economy was heading downhill. It came out of nowhere, and nobody knew what to do. Everyone I idolized in the real estate industry was panicking. The company I worked with was turned upside down almost overnight. I went from feeling as if I was in pursuit of my independence, to not knowing what to do all over again. I had worked so hard for what I had achieved, and suddenly I began questioning everything. All that work felt like such a waste. I had invested over two years of my life to become a real estate agent, and in less than two weeks it all came crashing down around me. I began thinking, "What am I going to do now? Do I need to move back home? What will everyone think of me?" I knew I didn't want to feel like a burden again. It felt like my freedom was being stripped away, and I was powerless to change it.

The market crash made me doubt my path. There were so many internal questions, but there was one that kept lingering, "What's next?" I knew I needed to figure something else out because that taste of freedom was so much better than feeling like a burden. A few weeks passed, and I ran into a friend who was also in the real estate business. He mentioned that he had started doing some work for banks. The banks needed help and although it was a kind of grunt work job, I realized it would put money in my pocket. The work was called Brokers Professional Opinion (BPO). These BPO jobs were big due to the market crash. What I did was help banks survey and assess a property that they were about to foreclose on.

The job was to provide my opinion on pricing for foreclosed properties to the bank. To do this I had to do market research and provide evidence that supported my opinion. It forced me to learn how to do research, and to become familiar with properties. I learned a lot about real estate through that job, but I didn't get to sell very much real estate, which is what I had intended to do. Although I was making money, I only used that money to support my bad habits, not to invest in anything that could advance my mission of independence. I was back to square one. Everything I had worked so hard for was not working out.

WORK ETHIC

I spent a lot of time feeling sorry for myself that year. I turned to drinking and smoking cigarettes, staying out all hours, and hanging out in different bars each night. During the day, I was doing BPOs, and at night I was a barfly. The one activity that took all my worries away and made me feel good was shooting pool (also known as billiards). I loved playing pool and had learned the game from my dad as a kid. It became my weekend hustle. I would take $20 and attempt to hustle someone out of $40. It wasn't the best use of my time, but it helped me cope with the loss of what I thought was my career. I didn't know it then, but these games taught me a lot about networking and connecting with people. I had to develop skills that allowed me to connect with just about anyone. I learned it was something I was very good at. It exposed a part of me I didn't know I had.

My late nights always ended with me hanging out with the bar manager or owners. I got to hear their stories and their experiences in running their business. This always fascinated me. It sparked an entrepreneurial spirit in me. One bar, in particular, became my go-to spot, and I spent the majority of my free time there. The owner of the business was also the manager and he and I became very close friends. He was involved in several other businesses, and I loved hearing about his businesses and what he was working on. He was truly a mentor without knowing it. After about a year of being a local there, I thought it would be a great idea to work there. But I was not content to be a bartender, I wanted to be a manager. I saw my friend, the owner, working really hard on other businesses and he wasn't able to give the attention to the bar that he needed to. I proposed that he should hire me to be the manager. He declined that proposition, and I assumed he thought I'd drink the profits. But I persisted and kept asking for several months until one day everything changed.

MY BIG SHOT

My friend, the bar owner, called me one day and asked if we could meet that night. I said yes since I knew I'd be there anyway. I thought he was going to ask me for a favor, I frequently helped him with paperwork, so I thought he had something big going on. I showed up that night willing to help with whatever my friend needed. Once we sat down, I could tell this time was going to be different. He shared some ongoing things in his other businesses and told me he realized that he needed to make a quick change. That change meant leaving the bar business. This was horrible for me because I loved that bar. Where would I go? He quickly followed that with, "David, I think you would be a great fit to become the new owner." I was shocked to hear this because he had never been interested in hiring me as a manager. I followed up with, "Yeah right I can't afford to do that." He went on to say, "Well, I can help." He then explained to me how he wanted me to take ownership of the business. I didn't believe him at first, but as he kept going, it became very clear to me that he was serious. I was still in shock, but I knew this was a big deal. I knew it would be literally life-changing for me. I accepted the offer, and in the next week, we started the transition.

I had been given the opportunity of a lifetime. I will share in future writing the exact details of the deal, but I want you to know I did it with no money down, and no money out of my pocket.

I didn't know what I was doing, and I had never run a business before, but I was willing to do it. It meant I was one step closer to freedom. Over the next two years, I learned how to run a business, which just happened to be a bar. I doubled the sales of the bar and built a very loyal following. To top it off, I was able to pay back the guy who had believed in me. I guess he thought I did such a good thing, he asked me to join him in his next business venture.

DAVID THE TAX MAN?

The next venture was extremely different from a bar. In fact, it was so different I wasn't convinced about it from the start. My partner who first believed in me thought it would be a good idea to get into the financial services industry, specifically the tax business. I thought this was a horrible idea! I told him the only thing I knew about taxes was, I don't like paying them. He explained in much more detail why he wanted to do this, and I finally gave in and agreed to hear more about it. The business was a franchise model, which meant we could go to an event where the franchisor would tell us everything we needed to know about the business and answer any questions we had. In truth, the only reason I agreed to go hear them out was that we were going to party in Dallas, TX. To my surprise, after attending the event, I became more interested in the business than I thought I would be. The fact that it was a tax business wasn't what got me interested, it was the people. I met so many people who were already working in this business from so many different backgrounds. All of them were experiencing life at a much higher level than I was. Honestly, they had what I had been seeking all my life, FREEDOM! That day, we decided to join Liberty Tax, the fastest-growing tax business in history.

Over the next few months, we opened our first tax office. This was not an easy task. I had never done 90% of the things we needed to do. I was challenged to work long hours and learn new things daily. I would work the tax business during the day, and the bar at night. I was literally working 20 hour days. Initially, I wondered how I found the strength and energy to do it. Where was this coming from? My friends and family would always check up on me, thinking I was going to die from working so hard. After several months I began to understand why I was able to flip the switch, so to speak, in my work ethic. It was because I had witnessed this kind of work ethic all my life. My parents were such hard-working people. They worked day in and day out. I can't remember a day where my parents just relaxed. If they were not at their jobs, they were working on the house or in the yard. They never stopped. Looking back, that was so impressive. They forced themselves to do whatever it took to get the job done and to ensure they didn't have to depend on anyone. My parents may have listened to the doctors and planned to take care of me all my life, but they themselves lived such an independent life their example was so much louder than their words. Their example led me to have that same work ethic.

January 2009 was my first tax season and with a lot of hard work, we finished ranking #4 out of 2,400 tax offices in the Liberty Tax system for revenue and production. I was finally feeling like independence and freedom were getting closer.

Just when I thought it was all coming together, life decided to throw another challenge my way. Back in 2006, my father was diagnosed with cancer. He battled cancer for 2 years and won. He was cancer-free. This was exciting news. It was a hard two years, and I saw the toll and stress this caused my parents. It was difficult, but it's what pushed me to figure out life. During those times, I saw their struggle and I didn't want to add to it by being a burden. My father was a strong man and I knew he could beat it and we thought he had. After my first tax season, my dad went for an annual check-up to ensure he was still cancer-free. At that visit, he was told cancer had come back. The battle against cancer was on. Again. This time was going to be different though. This time the treatments would require him to quit his job. The job that provided healthcare. Without healthcare, he was going to have to battle cancer alone. Battling cancer isn't cheap and my parents weren't rich. My parents had a savings account that had grown over time, but it wasn't much. I'm not sure how much they had managed to save, but I knew it wasn't enough to fight cancer. Over the next two years, my dad battled cancer with no healthcare and using only the money he had worked all his life to save. He eventually lost the battle and passed on in 2010, leaving behind nothing in savings for my mother, and no inheritance for our family.

FINDING FREEDOM

It was a hard loss, to say the least. Not only did I lose the man who raised me, but watching the effect his illness had on every aspect of life was eye-opening. My dad might still be here today if he hadn't run out of money. My dad might still be here today if he had healthcare. My dad might still be here today if he had watched his health. My dad lost so many years and opportunities to leave the legacy he deserved to leave.

This is the foundation of my path to writing this book. My parents taught me the importance of hard work and living an independent life. Although losing my dad was one of the toughest things I've ever endured, I knew something could be taken from this.

My life from that point forward was going to be focused on the pursuit of true freedom. I made the decision I would never allow the opinions or actions of others to influence the outcome of my life. My father had worked so hard to experience this, but he never got there, and it taught me such a great lesson. I used to think of an economy as just money! Now, I realize money is just one part of it. In fact, it's not money, it's wealth we should be thinking about. There's also no need for wealth if you don't have health. As the years passed, I witnessed so much. I knew moving forward, I would take a lesson from every experience so I could build the economy I deserved.

No matter your position in life, whether our stories are different or alike, I know it's possible for you too. Let me tell you how to achieve a life of health, wealth, success, and most importantly, freedom by building your own economy.

CHAPTER 1

DEFINING ECONOMIES

The word "economy" is a variation of the English word, "economics," which is derived from the Greek word "Oikonomia." It directly translates to "household management." The Greek Philosopher, Aristotle, deemed Economics as the science of household management. Essentially, an economy is how we use resources to fulfill the needs and wants of the people within a household. My definition of an Economy is how we use what we've been given to build a life that no circumstance can shake.

While it may be easy to think that the economy is something we have no control over, I don't believe that to be true, and neither should you. *Everything* is a choice. As architects of our own economies, we choose how to distribute resources to fulfill our needs, and in short, manage our household.

Although this book is primarily about your personal economy, it is very important to understand that there are other economies we may be involved in. Here are the 5 economies we can be involved in on a daily basis.

A **global** economy is an entire world.
A **national** economy is boiled down to countries or continents.
A **regional** economy is states or provinces.
A **local** economy is a city or county.
A **personal** economy is your own individual economy.
It's significant to understand the differences between these types of economies.

Throughout the book you will hear me refer to the outside economies, these are all economies except your own.

THE TYPE OF ECONOMY YOU ALLOW YOURSELF TO LIVE IN DETERMINES THE WAY YOU SEE THE WORLD.

If you participate in a global economy, every decision you make will be determined by what's happening on the global stage and the interactions between countries. Your reality will revolve around global forces.

If you participate in a national economy, you're defined by your country, and you make decisions based on national concerns, perhaps regarding border security, the war on drugs, or voting for the "right" government officials.

If you participate in a regional economy, you think about things that impact your state. For instance, you may consider how the state party majority, be it Republican or Democrat affects you.

If you participate in a local economy, you base your decisions on what's going on in your community, like natural disasters or other concerns within the limits of your city or county.

Then there's YOUR economy. If you participate in YOUR economy you are more concerned about the well-being of yourself, your family, and your loved ones. Your economy means you are committed to you first.

When your decisions are not swayed by factors that do not directly impact your well-being, you can begin to act in your own best interest and take control of your life. This is what this book is all about.

Now that you see the differences of each economy you must start to make a decision that being in your own economy is the most important. I'm advocating that you neglect all the rest of the economies. All play a vital role in your life, however, I do want you to first see how important it is that you focus on yours FIRST.

"MAKE YOURSELF A PRIORITY, IT'S NOT SELFISH IT'S REQUIRED."

ARE YOU REALLY IN CONTROL?

Before we can fully discuss control, we must first believe that we can only control ourselves. We have no control over anyone else or anything else, we can only control how we respond to everything outside of us. And, while we can't control what goes on in the White House, we can control what goes on in our own house.

There will always be a small few who sacrifice their lives to change things globally, regionally, nationally, or even locally. But for most of us, that's not how we choose to live. We choose to live for ourselves because we know that through our own economy true generational change happens.

To build your own economy you must keep in mind that there are factors that will impact your success or failure. These factors are the required resources to build. Think of them as the materials to build a home. Each plays a vital role in its structural soundness. These 4 factors are:

- Time
- Relationships
- Energy
- Money

When people start to lose control of these factors, they're not able to enjoy life or make impactful changes to better themselves or their position. If you allow outside forces to impact these factors you're not controlling your personal economy, and your life is essentially in the hands of another.

It's ironic. Believing that everything in the world impacts your decisions is the main reason people start to lose control of their economy. When you can separate your personal economy from the rest of the world, you can begin to take control over your life.

It's tough to get free from the mindset that everything affects you, but in reality, it is your choice whether something affects you or not. You have free will and the freedom to release what doesn't serve and doesn't affect you.

THE PROBLEM WITH HAVING THE FREEDOM TO CHOOSE IS THAT SOME PEOPLE WILL CHOOSE TO NOT BE FREE.

BUILDING YOUR OWN ECONOMY

So how do we choose freedom? The answer is by taking control of those **factors** that impact your economy. But what does that really mean? Well...

We've been taught all our lives that everything going on in the world is important and immediate. Whether you turn on the TV or open Facebook, there's always going to be a crisis, and you are always going to be told you should care about it. While staying informed and remaining engaged is important, it's even more important to separate these constant crises from your own economy.

TIME

Time is a nonrenewable resource, and if you waste it trying to fix others' problems instead of your own, you've lost control over one of the most important factors in your personal economy. You get to choose where your attention goes. It doesn't matter what the rest of the world is doing – the only thing you can control is yourself. You decide what you want to focus on.

ENERGY

When you use **energy** on another's economy, you're allowing them to profit from your losses and steal the vitality that you could use to build yours.

RELATIONSHIPS

It's easy to be distracted by other economies, whether they be global or even just that of another individual. When we start to invest in another economy, we often forget about our own. When we are more concerned about the **relationships** of other people or reality TV shows, we neglect and don't give attention to our own relationships. That's when problems arise. You can't control your personal economy while you're so engulfed in someone else's problems. For your economy to thrive, you must invest your time and energy into relationships that serve you.

MONEY

While **money** may be the basis of a transactional economy, it's only one factor of your personal economy. It is a very important one, however. You don't necessarily set your own pay, but you do decide what your time is worth and how many hours you work. You may not have the highest-paying job in the world, but you get to decide when to spend your money and when to save it. You can choose to control your buying patterns, and what is actually worth spending your hard-earned dollars on. To build your own economy, you need a lot of money.

Each of these factors will come into play as you start to build.

YOU DECIDE YOUR QUALITY OF LIFE

There are two types of people.
Those who decide to focus on their own economy.
Those who don't.

BUILDING YOUR OWN ECONOMY

We must decide which one we want to be. In fact, that's the beauty of life. We decide.

The people who build their own economy focus on themselves and the things they can control. And it's a daily decision that leads to a higher **quality of life.** If you want to enjoy your life, you need to practice being a student through life, not a follower. Most people don't understand there is a simple key to enjoying life, and that's taking control of it. At the end of the day, if you're not happy, you have nobody to blame but yourself.

I don't want to make it sound like it's impossible to build your own economy, but it will be a challenge. However, it has to be a decision every day because every choice we make is either benefiting our own economy or hurting it. **It's not easy, but it is worth it.** Either you're dictating your life or you have a dictator running your life. The choice is yours.

The importance of creating our own economy has never been more clear than during the year 2020. Globally, the world went through a pandemic and it influenced factors in every type of economy. It also stirred up a lot of negative emotions. As a country, and even globally, we turned to our governments to solve the problem. Most people decided to rely on public figures in the White House or famous doctors to fix the problems and tied their very lives to their success.

This is an example of the global economy telling us we need to surrender our independence and give up. So many people from all types of economies started to say "Hey, we didn't plan for this, we can't handle it, so let's depend on the government to take care of us." That was an easy way to opt out of their economy. They surrendered control. It may have seemed right at the time but what they neglected to realize is that no government can do the right thing for everyone. No one can solve everyone's problems. That's why we all need to have our own economy so that when something like a pandemic hits, you don't surrender, you thrive.

The government can't save the day or prevent illness from striking your family. They can't promise that an economic downturn won't hit you. Nothing can prevent an economic downturn in your life except for you, and even if you are in full control, mistakes can and will happen. Personally, I'd much rather understand and be able to say, "I'm the cause of my own problems." Otherwise, I'm just playing the victim. Taking responsibility for your own economy takes you from victim to victor.

When you find yourself needing to depend on someone else to provide for you, you have surrendered to an economy that is not your own. Once that happens, your money, time, energy, relationships, and quality of life are never going to be controlled on your own terms. Unforeseen circumstances can arise at any time, but if you continue to live within your own economy, you can react actively and maintain control over your own life.

CHAPTER 2

THE COMPONENTS THAT BUILD YOUR ECONOMY

Economy. It's a word we hear often, usually on the news or in our workplace. This seemingly intangible idea impacts our paychecks, careers, and quality of life. While it may seem that the economy is exclusively an outside force, affecting us in ways beyond our control, I would argue that you have more control over it than you might think.

> "LIFE IS NOT JUST THE PASSING OF TIME.
> LIFE IS THE COLLECTION OF EXPERIENCES
> AND THEIR INTENSITY." – JIM ROHN

Jim said it best, our lives simply put, are a collection of experiences. These experiences shape the way we think, act and live. This is very important to understand in order for us to move forward. You see, we are already programmed to see the world a certain way. Our perspective shapes how we live.

YOU DON'T KNOW WHAT YOU DON'T KNOW.

In 2008, I was a young aspiring realtor who had his hopes and dreams crushed by the crashing of the US Economy due to the collapse of the mortgage market. At the time, I had bet on myself doing great things through real estate, and I had invested a lot of time, energy, and money to get there. To see it all fall apart was very hard.

As I referenced in the introduction, in order to get through this tough time, I had to do things for banks to help them assess or evaluate properties that were going to be foreclosed on. I wasn't really excited about this job, but it was something I did to make money so I could feed my bad habits. At that time I didn't realize how impactful that job would be for me. Foreclosure happens when someone can't afford to pay their mortgage anymore, and the bank has to come back in and say, "Hey, you promised to pay us. If you can't afford to pay us, we're going to have to kick you out and take this property back." Now, in a right and wrong world, taking a property back makes financial sense, but I quickly began to understand both sides of the equation. Deep down inside, nobody wants people to be homeless or see them get kicked out of their homes. I was young back then, so I didn't really understand how important this was. I just took it as a job, and a way to survive.

Looking back, this was my first encounter with building an economy. I saw hundreds of families being torn away from their homes, and when I say families, I really mean there were kids involved. I saw parents having to tell their kids, "This isn't your room anymore. This isn't our house anymore." That has to be one of the hardest things any parent would have to tell their child. While this was hard for them, it was easy for me. I went in there and evaluated each property, "This is what it's worth." Then I was on to the next.

Now, I can see this is where it all started for me. I saw so many people going through challenging times and, at the time, I thought it was their fault. I really did. I remember thinking, "Man, these guys are dumb. They should have just paid their bills. They shouldn't have lost their jobs. They should have known what they were getting themselves into." I was naive. I didn't really understand that, in some respects, it wasn't their fault. Did they play a part in what happened? Of course. Their decisions had something to do with it, but those beautiful people were sold an idea of homeownership. They were sold the idea by a banker, a realtor, a mortgage lender, a family member, a friend, a community group, an organization, or a nonprofit. Everybody was pushing the agenda, "Go buy a home!" Lenders were willing to lend anybody money to buy a home. If they could breathe, they got a loan. Back then, they called them NINJA loans, which stands for "No income, no job, and no assets". These loans were approved, no matter the circumstances. Many people were sold this idea and they bought into it. They got a house and most were put on interest rate programs that were variable. That means their interest rate was tied to the performance of the national economy. Basically, that meant their payment could fluctuate. Depending on how their loan was structured (and there's a lot more complexity to it) a person's mortgage payment could have been $500 one month, and the next month it could have been $1,000 a month. If you're like me, when you sign up for a bill and they tell you an amount, you budget for that and that should be it. No one saw it coming.

These families were in a position where they couldn't afford to make their payments after their interest rate had been adjusted. Now because of these variable adjustments, they were going to lose their homes. I was there to figure out how much the bank could sell those homes for because the bank wanted its money. By the way, that's how many banks went bankrupt. Too many people said, "Here. Take the house back!" Initially, the banks had a lot of money to lend out, but now they couldn't get any of it back because nobody could buy the houses that had been foreclosed on. Lots of supply but no demand. This is a topic for another book. Several years later, I came to realize that it was more than a job to me. It exposed me to the ways people can be controlled. Many people went through that economic downturn, and for some of them, what happened was really no fault of their own, except for the fact that they agreed to make the payments. They were sold an agenda by many other people, and an idea of homeownership that wasn't really sustainable.

What they bought into improved someone else's economy. Somebody else was getting rich, while they were going broke. Somebody else was buying real estate, while they were losing theirs. Someone else was succeeding, while they were losing.

I REALIZE NOW THAT THE PEOPLE WHO SUCCEEDED THE MOST DURING THIS DOWNTURN WERE THE PEOPLE WHO CONTROLLED THEIR OWN ECONOMY.

Some people went through the 2008 economic downturn and made a killing, a fortune, and built wealth, while others went through 2008 and drowned. They came out financially bankrupt. The difference between the two individuals is very clear to me. Some had a plan, and some didn't. Some thought through their decisions, and some didn't.

As much as I'd like to tell you that it was their fault or that they deserved it because they made those decisions, and they signed the promissory notes to pay for those homes, and that they knew what they were getting into, a lot of them didn't. It's truly a sad statement because, if you're controlling your own economy, or building your own economy, that means you should not have to worry about losing your home, your livelihood, or your family. It means you shouldn't ever have to go home and tell your family, "We have to go. This isn't our house anymore."

Back then, I didn't understand what was really happening. Now, when I look back, I remember seeing so many people in so much pain. I witnessed so much loss from all of this.

It's not something I wish upon you. Losing anything you love is painful.

Let me tell you here and now, this book is going to show you how to build your own economy so that no bank can take your home, and no person can shake you down financially. You will become a wealth-health-principle-legacy-focused person. Reading this book will show you how to do it.

YOUR FUTURE COULD BE YOURS.

Imagine we live in a world where we aren't worried, stressed, or fearful of what could happen to us. How freeing would that be? What could we accomplish if we weren't restrained by our own self-imposed limitations? Safety, security, protection, and peace of mind. Those are things I believe we all deserve to have, and that's exactly what building your own economy does.

Before we can move forward, I should warn you. It won't be easy for you to take full control of your life and design the economy you deserve. You'll need to take full ownership of where you are today and free yourself from the past. This book is based on a rule I live by: I am the cause and the solution to all my current problems. No one else is to blame.

JUST LIKE DRIVING A CAR, YOU ALWAYS CONTROL THE DIRECTION. IF YOU CRASH, IT'S NO ONE'S FAULT BUT YOUR OWN.

Let's begin with first seeking to understand how we start taking ownership of our lives. Just as in the driving example, you get to

BUILDING YOUR OWN ECONOMY

control the direction of your life. If you didn't control the direction, you'd get in the passenger seat and go along for the ride. Sadly, this is the way many people live their lives, in the passenger seat. This is what I'll call: living in someone else's economy.

You see, building and then living in your own economy allows you to control the speed, direction, and destination. You can also decide who comes along for the ride. It's your journey.

Many of my childhood years were spent in the passenger seat. This may be taken literally, as I couldn't drive as a child, but most of my childhood was spent surrendering to the opinions of others. Growing up labeled as "special needs" was very comfortable. Everyone from my family and my teachers had my safety and security in mind. There was always someone around to "TAKE CARE OF ME."

A good example of this was when it was time for recess. During recess, all the kids got to go outside and play in the playground. I, however, had to sit in the classroom playing with cards while I watched the other kids having fun through the window. I remember always wishing I could join them, but I couldn't. The teachers knew that if I went outside, I'd get sunburned and my mom would be very upset. Being protected always felt good, but looking back, it really messed me up!

You see, not being able to go outside wasn't really what messed me up. It was me being coddled. I was given a false sense of security at a young age. I was sheltered and protected from the sun and the world.

As a child growing up with albinism, I got a lot of special treatment. I got to skip lines and received extra attention. It felt like there was always someone there to take care of anything I needed. It seemed like a perfectly fine way to go about life, except during recess when I wasn't allowed outside to play. The lack of pigment in my skin meant that I would sunburn easily, so I was forced to sit inside and watch as the other kids laughed and ran through the playground. I wasn't able to fully comprehend it then, but I started to realize in some small way that I wasn't going to have much of a life if that life was always going to be controlled by someone else. I began to become frustrated with the notion that my life was not my own to live.

YOU CAN'T SLEEP AT NIGHT IF YOU'RE ANGRY WITH SOMEONE ELSE, BUT YOU CAN IF YOU'RE ONLY UPSET WITH YOURSELF.

In my teens, I was faced with the reality that I'd lost so much of my childhood by not speaking up. At the time, I thought it was a privilege to be coddled and corralled, but the fact of the matter is, I would have preferred to play on the playground, even if it meant getting burned. Now, I try to foster that independent spirit in my own life, with my family. Encouraging the freedom of choice for those you love is a gift to them because a life of dependence isn't a life anyone really wants to live. It's better they live life to the fullest and on their own terms.

That's the risk you run when you take control of your economy. Maybe you fly too close to the sun and get burned, but isn't that better than never feeling its warmth at all? Freedom is the key. So how do you achieve it? Well...

I believe that freedom is a state of mind. Our circumstances can act as a prison, limiting our choices, abilities, and options, but we always have control over our thoughts and actions within those confines. Take, for example, Mahatma Gandhi. He was a prisoner of war held captive for many years, but in that captivity, he found inner peace, and he became one of the most influential people in the world. When he was finally released, he created a movement of unity and peace in the Middle East and India.

Some circumstances are beyond your control. Perhaps you have a prison of your own in some way, whether that be the position into which you were born or limitations imposed upon you. In those cases, your freedom can be found in your own mind, and you might be surprised what shackles fall away when you free your mind.

So how do you escape the proverbial prison of your life? How do you create a mindset that can lead to a personal revolution? It starts with finding your freedom....

THE 4 COMPONENTS OF AN ECONOMY

There are four components that form your personal economy: **Rules, Health, Wealth, and Legacy.** Simply put, these are the four aspects of your life in which you must achieve freedom before you can reap the benefits of your personal economy. When you decide to free yourself from another's economy in each of these categories, only then can you enjoy the peace of mind that comes from living within your own economy.

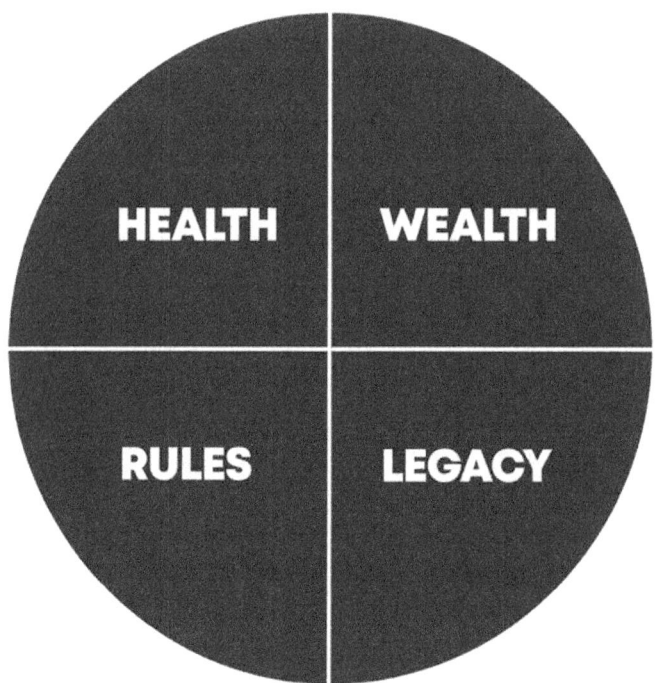

LET'S BREAK THEM DOWN.

YOUR RULES (VALUES & PRINCIPLES)

Rules: one set of explicit principles guiding your decision making. Each one of us has rules that we live by – whether we know it or not.

HEALTH

Health is more than just looks. To be truly healthy, you must understand that the inside is more important than the outside of our bodies. When you don't have good **health**, you have to depend on family, doctors, specialists, and other people to support you on how to live your life. Caring for your health is a key component of independence, and building your own economy.

WEALTH

Wealth is much more than money, but in this book, I will refer to it as a means for acquiring a lifestyle on your own terms. Not having enough money is a problem.

If you don't have enough money, you may have to depend on someone to provide for you. If someone must provide for you, you lack independence. Not everyone is born with money, but everyone can find a way to make it. To truly master our own economy and achieve freedom, we must position ourselves to achieve financial independence.

LEGACY

Your legacy is what you will leave behind and are remembered for. When we die, we want to leave a **positive** impact on the world. If you build your own economy, you leave generational wealth, you leave an impact on people's lives, you create joy and memories that will carry your name. If you don't focus on building your legacy each day, you will be remembered by no one.

Keep these four components in mind as we go through the book. Each of them will be referenced in much greater detail in the coming chapters. Your goal is to master each one and find ways to be very conscious of how they impact your current economy.

CHAPTER 3

A FOUNDATION OF FREEDOM

We've identified the various types of economies and their components. It's important to know which economy you're living in. Living in your own economy is the best, but why is that so important?

If I had to sum it up in one word, it would be the word *"freedom."* Freedom isn't just about being free, it's about having options. Freedom is our ability to not let anything outside of us control us. You see, I believe the world is always out to control us. Something is always trying to grab our attention, to make us think a certain way, or to make us do certain things. For example, during the 2020 pandemic, all economies were impacted all around the globe.

This was a true test for those of us who have taken our own economies into our own hands. You see, the world in 2020 seemed to be coming to an end. The rapid spreading of a virus called COVID-19 had everyone in fear. This virus was predicted to be one of the deadliest viruses to ever hit our world. This virus attacked the lungs, the heart, as well as people's sense of taste and smell. It was a vicious virus, and for too many, this virus was deadly. Our country, and many other countries across the world, shut down. Our economies were struck hard financially. Many businesses couldn't operate. Many people couldn't go to work. Many homes were filled with sick and scared people. Our hospitals were overrun with patients who were victims of this virus. No one knew what to do.

This was a challenge for many people, including myself. When we're faced with something new, something unknown, most people will become paralyzed, sometimes for hours, weeks, or months.

We were told by the media and our governments to stay inside. Shelter in place, protect yourself at all costs. Many people were scared, fearful, and worried about not only themselves but about their community, their families, and the people around them. We practiced social distancing and wore masks. We hid from each other for several months, in the hope that we could prevent this virus from spreading and to avoid contracting it. This was one of the toughest times in most people's lives. And we were all alone. It was in some respects every man for himself.

This was a very, very good time for those of us who had chosen to live and build our own economies. Guys like me went through this pandemic, not scared, not fearful, but brave and confident. Personally, I took this as a sign that I now had an opportunity to get ahead while everyone was sitting back, scared, and hiding in a corner. I'm not just talking about getting ahead financially, there is a lot more to it.

IF YOU UNDERSTAND THE FOUR COMPONENTS OF AN ECONOMY, YOU ALSO UNDERSTAND THAT THERE ARE A FEW THINGS YOU CAN DO IN A PANDEMIC OR OTHER CRISIS.

First, I understood that it was important to not lose focus on the **rules** that guided my decisions. I relied heavily on my values and principles to ensure I was in alignment with those rules. During the pandemic, I became more clear on the rules that guided me. Here are some examples.

- My health is the most important thing in my life. Without my health, I can help no one!
- The health and wealth of my family is the number one priority in my life today.
- When other people are fearful. I will be brave.
- When the outside economy is crashing. I will be building.
- I will be positive when others are negative.
- I will support causes that support those who don't live in their own economy, but I will always be mindful of my own.
- I will be a student through tough times, not simply a follower.

Next, I didn't believe the virus would be deadly to me. This was me believing in my health. That's what helped me to not fear it. Before the pandemic, I had already made the decision to prioritize my **health.** I realized that my health was under my own control, and decided I wasn't going to allow my health to be sacrificed by anything in any way. In entering a pandemic that had the potential to impact my health, I entered knowing I was strong mentally and physically. I knew my health was good and that I could fight this virus.

Then, we move on to **wealth.** During the pandemic, businesses had to shut down, and I'm a business owner. Many people were very fearful that they were going to lose their businesses, that they were going to have to shut their doors, and probably file for bankruptcy. I was very fortunate, in that before this pandemic, I had already made a decision to control my own wealth. I had several companies and passive investments that continued to pay me throughout the pandemic. In fact, in the year 2020, I made more money than I'd ever made before. It wasn't because of COVID, it was because I was living in my own economy. During a time where many people were living in the "national" economy or the "global" economy, I was working on my own economy.

And lastly, I constantly reminded myself throughout the pandemic that the decisions I made now would ultimately define my **legacy**. I didn't want to leave behind a memory of fear and uncertainty. I wanted to be known as brave, strong, expansive and committed to getting through it better than when I went in. I kept thinking of my unborn children and how they would be impacted by my decisions.

I left that pandemic better than when I went in. In fact, my health was even better than when it started. I had more wealth than I'd ever had in my life. In 2020, I have gotten a clear understanding of what my legacy should be. Most importantly, I had clearly defined some rules that I want to instill in my children and those around me. It felt so good knowing that my own economy had gotten stronger.

PEACE OF MIND

What will your economy create for you? The answer is simple – safety, security, and freedom. What I love best, though, is **peace of mind.** It can only come from existing in your own economy. Peace of mind comes from eliminating our anxiety of the unknown. When we're scared, it's typically because we don't know what's going to happen. So many people go through life living with fear, because, "What if I get laid off?" "What if I get COVID-19?" "What if, God forbid, something happens to me?" Because of this, we have a mindset that anything and everything *could* go wrong. How do we reconcile that fear? Well, building an economy gives you peace of mind when you can say, *"Everything that happens to me is my own fault."*

When you understand that everything is your own fault, it changes everything. Personally, it has made me a better person. When I realized that I was responsible for my actions as well as their outcomes, when I stopped blaming the world for my problems and I started to take responsibility, my worries began to dissipate. I started making better decisions with more confidence. You can too.

Though it may not sound appealing, realizing everything that happens is your fault, is actually incredibly **freeing**. When you take control of your life, your actions, and their results, fear, and anxiety become a thing of the past. You begin to live life by design and not by chance. You have no anger toward anyone or anything because you stop the blame game. You sleep better at night knowing you're where you are now because *you* brought yourself there. Nobody else.

"WE ARE ALL SELF-MADE BUT ONLY THE SUCCESSFUL WILL ADMIT IT." – EARL NIGHTINGALE

I want to build a life, I don't want to be surprised by life. I want peace of mind. If you do too, you really must build your own economy.

BEING IN CONTROL

Often people see the word **control** as being a negative aspect of their lives, but I challenge you to think about it differently. Many of us want control, usually over others. We want control over our children, career, money, and our lives in general. However, many people do not really understand that in order to have control they have to exercise discipline. Discipline is training yourself to **do the things you know you NEED to do,** not simply those you want to do.

BUILDING YOUR OWN ECONOMY

When you take control of your life you will start seeing the world differently. Suddenly, the world isn't out to get you. You stop being a victim and you start being a victor. **I believe the world is full of victims looking to blame someone for their unfortunate circumstances.**

In many cases, that's why there's so much drama and confusion in the world today. So many people are blaming everybody else for their problems. Rather than focusing on their own economy, they invest in others. Then, they try to blame other people for the circumstances they created themselves. Sometimes, they even try to control others, thinking it will somehow impact their economy. They're spinning their wheels attempting to control things they have no control over.

It's important to think about and understand what you actually have control of, essentially your own thoughts, and your own actions. You can't control other people. However, if you control your own economy, you control your health, your wealth, your legacy, and write your own rules.

Think of it like voting. Let's say you go out and vote with your heart for a candidate you support. Then, let's say that candidate doesn't win. Well, it would be easy to get upset. But, that would be useless because the whole thing is out of my control. At least you know you voted for your beliefs. If you voted, and you voted for what you believed in, then you did your part. You took control of your own life and released the desire to control something you can't. And that's peace of mind to me because I created it.

WRITING YOUR OWN PAYCHECK

I believe people have the opportunity to write their own paycheck and to secure their own financial future. Once you make the decision to give something your all, you may decide to show up early or stay late, so you can make sure the job gets done right. And because of those decisions, you control your outcome. You may even make the decision to walk away from a job that doesn't meet your expectations. If you work hard and give it your all, you can have peace of mind knowing there are no regrets. The world will reward your efforts. If I go out and work, I know I'm going to get a reward. It may not be the reward I want, but at least I'm getting rewarded for my efforts.

THE WORLD WILL PAY YOU FOR WHAT YOU'RE WORTH, NOT A PENNY MORE.

If you don't control your own economy, somebody's going to control you. They'll try to control your destiny, your fate, and your outcome. They'll write your paycheck, and they'll become your boss. This doesn't mean working for a company is wrong. In fact, I believe working for a company can truly benefit your economy. What I want you to know is that your efforts are directly benefiting you, not a company. You are always going to be an independent contractor in life. No one can keep you employed against your will. Your decision to work there is a decision of your own, not a necessity. If you work for a company out of necessity, you are not in control of your own economy.

BUILDING YOUR OWN ECONOMY

Controlling your own outcome is the most important thing. That's why building a personal economy is important.

ASK YOURSELF A FEW QUESTIONS:

- Do you want to be at the mercy of others or the master of your own destiny?
- Do you want to be worried about what could happen, or confident in your actions and owner of the outcome?
- Do you want to be controlled, or be in control?
- Personally, I'd rather be in complete control of my future by knowing I have mastered the 4 components of my economy.

Think of a strong personal economy as a never-ending circle surrounding you and protecting you from outside economies. The whole point of creating an economy of your own is to protect you against anything that would happen to you and your family.

Your personal economy is the one thing that you must protect, defend, create, develop and control every single day. I believe this so strongly. If you don't do this, you'll fall into someone else's economy. When that happens, you're dependent on someone else in some way, shape, or form. You will never be truly free living this way.

CHAPTER 4

DEFINING YOUR MINDSET

Before we begin this chapter, I would like to reference something very important moving forward. Any time you aren't in complete control of a decision that impacts your life, you are not living in your own economy.

Building your own economy takes time, hard work, and consistency. However, not only is it something that everyone is capable of, it's the only way you should live.

MINDSET SHIFT

In building your personal economy, you have to start with the right mindset. Mindset is kind of a buzzword, and many people use the word without truly knowing what it means. Webster's Dictionary defines Mindset as "an established set of attitudes held by somebody." The most important word in that definition is *attitudes*. An attitude, defined by Webster's is, "a settled way of thinking, as reflected in one's behavior." When you hear the word mindset, it's really **the attitude you have toward life**. If you're thinking about building your own economy, which you are if you're reading this book, you need to have the right mindset. This is the biggest challenge we all face before we can build our own economy.

"YOUR ATTITUDE, NOT YOUR APTITUDE, WILL DETERMINE YOUR ALTITUDE" – ZIG ZIGLAR.

Your attitude toward anything in life doesn't really have a lot to do with you. It has everything to do with the environment you're in, and the environment you come from. There's an old adage, **"You are who you hang out with,"** and I believe it's very true. Most people don't actually have their own thoughts. Everything they do is influenced by what their parents taught them or comes from the community they live in, the media, their church, or their friends. In other words, the economy they are in is mostly determined by the people they associate with.

Sometimes, we suppress our own mindset to fit in. We may actually know what's right and what's wrong, not in a legal sense, but for example: we know what foods promote good health and which don't... Most of the time, however, we don't listen to ourselves because we're more influenced by the outside economies. We're more influenced by what our friends and families think than we are from ourselves. This is why it's very hard to change your mindset. You have to decide to become the person you really want to be and stop giving a crap about what those around you think..

Building Your Own Economy isn't about anyone else but you.

Let's start by asking a few questions to help you shift your mindset and promote a shift in attitude.

WHERE ARE YOU RIGHT NOW?

The first step is seeing where you are currently. This isn't easy at first. Someone once told me that a great characteristic of a leader is being able to see themselves as they really are. Many people see themselves as worse than they are. I believe this is because we are all inherently negative. It's difficult to see the good in everything. We all tend to remember the bad things and tend to forget the good things.

A good example of this would be me growing up with Albinism. I have referenced this quite often because it reminds me of how negatively I used to view myself. All the other kids used to make fun of me. They picked on me, called me silly names, that hurt my feelings. Growing up, I took those memories with me. I was shy and afraid of what people would think about me. I worried about how others would see me. Going into my teens and early 20s, that's who I was. I still carried that negativity with me.

MY SHIFT

In my mid-20s, I realized attention is what people need in life if they intend to do great things. One of my mentors, Michael Burt, says all the time: "You don't need more money, you need more people." This really means you need to be known by lots of people in order for you to build your own economy.

Think of anyone who is known in the world by many people. They get attention which gets them paid. "Good or bad press" as they say, is better than no press at all. For me, that meant turning that negativity into a positive. I had to embrace who I was and what I looked like. I knew I was different, instead of trying to fit in, I needed to work harder on standing out. I turned it all around. I know now that no matter where I go or what I do, people don't forget me. I stick out like a sore thumb!

MINDSET ASSESSMENT

WHERE ARE YOU CURRENTLY?

On a scale of 1-10

Control in your life? _____
Your health _____
Your wealth _____
Your legacy _____
Clearly defined rules _____

If any of your grades are below 8, this is an area of focus that you must work on. Visit my website to take a more in-depth assessment to help determine ways to improve each component of your economy.

WHO DO YOU WANT TO BE?

I'm a strong believer in starting with the end in mind. We can't show up each day without having a clearly defined outcome. It's like driving to somewhere you've never been before without a map hoping that you'll just accidentally find your destination.

It may sound strange, but the next step in a mindset shift is deciding **who you want to be**. Some people will say, "I want to be the best I can be!" Well, that's great, but we need to get below surface-level things. It's hard to get past the cliche stuff, "I want to be good." "I want to be a nice person." "I want to be happy." The real answer is much deeper. You have to be really detailed in your responses, and this is where the mindset shift comes.

Example:

"I want to be a great parent." This is said by anyone who either has or wants to have a child. The simple statement has no real meaning unless you clearly define it. It would be better to ask:

"What does a great parent look like?"

Sample Answer:

"A great parent supports their child financially, physically, spiritually, and emotionally. They are there when their child needs them and they make every decision with the intent to provide more opportunity than was afforded to them. A great parent is a role model and not a friend."

This would be very similar to goal setting. Many people make very loose statements like:

"I want to lose weight." This can be said by MILLIONS of people across the world. This is a simple statement but it doesn't give you any real goal or way to measure success.

A better statement:

"I want to lose 20 pounds so I can take back control of my health. The 20 pounds I need to lose will allow me to be more active in the lives of my children and more confident in my career."

So ask yourself the following:

Who do you want to be?
Why do you want to be this person?
What benefits come from being this person?

WHAT STEPS DO YOU NEED TO TAKE TO BE THIS PERSON?

Once you've got an idea about who you want to be, the next step is writing down what you have to do (or avoid doing) to become that person. This is often the hardest part.

We all inherently want things to stay the same, and that's what many refer to as "the comfort zone." We feel comfortable when we feel certain about the outcomes. That's why most people have trouble eating at different restaurants or shopping at different stores. They know what they're getting when they go to the same places. **Staying comfortable is the enemy of becoming the person you were meant to be.**

To start, you'll have to make a commitment. This commitment is not to me or anyone else, it's to yourself. You will have to make decisions that will guide you towards becoming the person you want to be. The best way to start this is by asking yourself questions.

"THE IMPORTANT THING IS TO NOT STOP QUESTIONING."
– ALBERT EINSTEIN

Here are some examples:

Wealth is part of the person you want to become, you could ask, "How would a wealthy person act? What do wealthy people do with their money? What is a habit that most wealthy people have?" If you aren't sure of the answers, Google search or YouTube search the topic of wealth.

I remember going through an exercise at a Tony Robbins event a few years ago. He had us work through this to better understand how questions and commitment work together.

BUILDING YOUR OWN ECONOMY

THIS IS WHAT WE DID – TAKE OUT A SHEET OF PAPER AND FOLLOW ALONG.

Imagine a young single you. Before you got married or into a relationship. Think back at the dream partner you wanted in your life. Take the opportunity to draw him/her up on a paper and list out all the things you wanted them to be/have. Now imagine going to find them. "If you really want to find the perfect person, your soulmate, write down what that person looks like. Write down what kind of person they are. Be detailed! How tall would they be? How smart? What kind of lifestyle would they have? What kind of parent would they be? Do they have kids? What kind of things do they like to do?"

We each wrote pages of details about our perfect person. For me, it described the person I'd want to marry.

In the end, Tony said, "The perfect person is definitely out there and has all the attributes and qualities you wrote down. But, if this perfect person was standing right in front of you, would they want you?" **WOW, this was a big statement.**

Well, 99% of the time (maybe even 100%) the answer would be no. Why? She wouldn't want me because I didn't embody many of the things on my own list. If I'm not perfect, I can't expect her to be perfect. If I said she had to be in shape, I needed to be in shape. If I said she had to be faithful, I need to be faithful. If I said she had to like to read, I need to like reading. People are attracted to people who share the same beliefs.

I had never thought of things this way before. So I had to actually be all the things on my list, or I would have to settle for whoever I could find. And that's how people end up settling in life, not living a life by design but a life in someone else's economy.

If we truly want a great life, we have to work to be great every day. If we settle for being average and expect to get above-average results, it's never going to happen. You can't think, "I'm never going to meet my person, they don't exist." Oh, they exist. They just don't like you. They don't want you because you don't fit what they're looking for.

It's the same concept with a mindset shift. You can't expect to go through life the same way you are today, and still expect to build your own economy. You have to be purposeful and intentional. You do that by focusing on all the components of an economy.

INDECISION IS A HORRIBLE PLACE TO LIVE.

WHEN DO YOU INTEND TO START TAKING THESE STEPS?

Now is the time to make a decision. Are you going to make a shift or are you going to stay where you feel comfortable? You are going to have to make a decision sooner or later, my recommendation, do it NOW!

I believe most people will stay in what I'll call an indecision zone. The Indecision zone paralyzes you. It steals opportunity. It steals time. Imagine sitting at home all day, wanting to write a book, but never writing it. That's indecision; a dead end. We all will eventually die, knowing this means you must do as much as you can while you are here.

WHEN WILL NOW BE THE RIGHT TIME?

There should be a reason strong enough to make you change. What is it for you? Maybe it's a lifestyle you desire, or a family you must support. Maybe you're just fed up with living in indecision.

I think there's a deep-seated purpose and reasoning behind everything we do in life, but we're all hardwired from past experiences. You bring those past experiences with you into the present, but you have a choice. You can either use them as a crutch or as a tool. Then, those experiences either become **limiting beliefs** or **empowering beliefs**. One or the other is going to happen. I guarantee it. The difference between those who control their own economy and those who don't is: if they believe in themselves. Those who control their own economy have empowering beliefs that support their decisions.

For example, my belief system tells me nobody went to college in my family, so nobody ever will. We're all idiots. We all suck at math. So, I could say all that and I would be limited by it. Or, I could say, "Hey, nobody's done it yet, but

I can be the first one." I want to be the first, so I'm going to go take on the challenge. That's turning a limiting belief into an empowering one.

I believe **progress equals happiness**. When people fall in love with progress, they embrace change.

A note to keep in mind.

This isn't a concept on how to be happy and excited to get up in the morning every single day. Some days will be hard, and that's okay. As long as you know you're in control, it makes you feel like any challenge can be overcome. We're all going to be faced with challenges. You might as well make the decision to tackle them on your own terms. Do this today, because you're going to go through challenges whether you control your economy, or if you don't. **The difference is the way in which you find a solution. If you're living in your own economy, *you have the solution*. We may not be happy every single day, but you can certainly be satisfied with the progress you make every single day.**

IF YOU MAKE THE CHOICE TO START BUILDING YOUR PERSONAL ECONOMY, YOU'RE MAKING A CHOICE TO BUILD AN UNSHAKEABLE LIFE.

Repeat after me: "I don't want to be rich today. I want to be rich forever. I don't want to be healthy today. I want to be healthy forever. I want to have values and principles I live by that guide my whole life, not just today. I want to be able to put plans into action and find happiness in the progress I make every single day. I don't want to go to the roller coaster and just put my hands up and just say let's go. I want to set the direction, the course, and speed. I want to be the architect of my own life."

When you actually understand you have core values you must live by, when you act like your health is just as important as the money you generate, you've made progress, and you're happy. When you do generate money or wealth that continues to grow to see future generations, and you bring that together with your faith, life becomes magical. It's freedom at its finest. Getting better every day, seeing yourself grow, and building something long-lasting. It's the ultimate satisfaction.

BELOW ARE THE RESULTS FROM MY ASSESSMENT

WHERE ARE YOU CURRENTLY?

On a scale of 1-10

How do you currently feel about control in your life? 7
Your health 8
Your wealth 7
Your legacy 8

WHO DO YOU WANT TO BE?

I want to be the man that looks in the mirror and says: "I did everything I could with the resources I had. I want to be a role model to those around me and provide an unshakeable foundation to my family. I want to leave the world better than I found it. I want to build so much wealth that it impacts 5 generations. I want to contribute to the world".

WHAT STEPS DO I NEED TO TAKE TO BE THIS PERSON?

I need to remind myself daily of who I need to become. I will maximize my resources by ensuring I invest my time based on my rules. I need to invest my money into assets that are tangible. I need to have a focus on contributions because I know that will live beyond my lifetime. I need to structure a legacy wealth transition plan that incentives my future generations to share the principles I do.

WHEN DO YOU INTEND TO START TAKING THESE STEPS?

Right now! Working on this book is part of my legacy. I will make only decisions today that are based on the rules I set, regardless of my emotions.

CHAPTER 5

BUILDING YOUR RULES

If you want to have control over your own personal economy, first, let me tell you what **_not_ to do.**

Leave everything to chance. Wait around for things to happen. Avoid problems. Count on luck and happenstance.

What you'll get is a life that's characterized by chaos and randomness. By living like that, you won't build your economy. But, if you, like me, want a life run by no one but yourself, you'll need some rules to follow.

In this chapter, I will refer to rules as the guiding values and principles that direct your decisions.

A value is something you deeply believe in.

A principle is something that guides you to that value.

A rule is a set of explicit or understood regulations or principles governing conduct within a particular activity or sphere.

Simply put, values are your beliefs and principles and putting those beliefs into action. In your economy, these ideals will dictate not only how you should live your life, but help you to achieve the life you want to live. Before we move forward, I ask that you always reference the person you want to become, not the person you currently are. This will help to develop the rules that guide you in the direction you want.

Almost everyone has values and principles in some way. People know what matters to them but rarely do they clearly identify those ideals and put them into practice in the form of actions. We sometimes don't know how to explicitly elaborate or articulate those values or principles, and that's not going to get you very far. **So many people go through life without clearly understanding what they value, or what their principles are.** They act on impulse, without thought or reference to their values, and those actions create not only an out-of-balance belief system but an unproductive and ultimately unfulfilling life.

If honesty is one of your values, your principles should be truth and transparency. You must always keep in mind those principles to guide your actions, and behave as an honest person does. Solidifying those belief systems allows you to use them as a compass, and make the path to the life you want to live and the person you want to be.

How do you clearly define your values? How do you decide on the principles that lead you to these values? Well, you start with the end in mind.

Let me ask you a question.

What do you want people to say about you when you're gone? Maybe you want them to say, "He was funny." "They were always smiling." "She was smart." "He was a giver." "They were creative." "He was honest." "She was committed." "They were successful." "She was rich." "They were healthy." Whatever you want people to say about you, you must start living that now.

Another example.

Let's say you choose to value honesty. Lots of people do. You want people to say, "He was always an honest man." How do you go from valuing honesty to principled action in a way that will guide you and ensure that people *will* remember you as that? Saying you value honesty is the easy part. Actually living your life being honest under all circumstances takes determination and dedication on your part. Once you decide honesty is truly important, every decision you make from then on should take that value into account. If you have a decision to make, even if you know being honest will hurt someone's feelings, you must say what needs to be said. Some people say they value honesty, but then behave dishonestly when it serves them. Instead of referencing those values and principles, they opt for the easy choice.

When building your own economy, I challenge you to solidify your core values and beliefs and use those principles to guide your decisions and actions. If you value financial security, don't spend half your paycheck on drinks and food every weekend. Those actions speak to a system of thought that values materialism and indulgence over security, and your economy will not be in alignment with your values.

None of us were born with a value system. These are learned ideas. What we value and the principles we follow are developed through action and experience, and through witnessing other's behaviors. Many times they're instilled in us by our parents.

Growing up, my parents were hard workers. My mom would get up at five o'clock every morning to make me breakfast and prepare for the work day. She would drop me off at school or with my aunt, then drive to work to be there by 7 AM. She'd work till 6 PM, then come home to cook dinner, clean the house, and iron my clothes. On weekends, she helped my father work on the house. The home we lived in wasn't the dream house they pictured. My parents bought a fixer-upper because that's all they could afford. They committed to making it their dream home themselves. I can't remember a weekend where they just relaxed. I don't think they knew what that word meant. They were machines. I witnessed this all my life.

I didn't realize until my twenties what they were doing. I just thought this was normal, just the way of the world. But, I realized it was the farthest thing from "normal." I saw them work really hard all the time. It wasn't because they were trying to get ahead, they were just working hard because that's all they knew how to do.

During all my time at home, they never asked me to step in and do a damn thing. I was spoiled because I was "special." I wasn't asked to help my dad put up wood siding on the house. I wasn't asked to get in the kitchen and cook, or to clean the house either.

I was "special." The doctor said so. My parents listened.

As I matured and entered the "real world" as they say, I started my first career as a real estate agent. I just assumed I would find and hire people who could do all those things I was never asked to do. I thought it would be easy to get someone to put up signs, fill out paperwork and take care of my calls. I quickly realized that wasn't how it was going to be. I didn't realize how easy I had it. It started to all make sense.

One day it all came together. I realized that if I wanted to do better I had to do it myself. And I became a workaholic. And I don't mean smart work, I mean grunt work. In my real estate business, I was the one who was typing up the paperwork, doing my own filing, taking the pictures, and making the phone calls. Although I wasn't as efficient, organized, or proficient as I could have been, I came to realize that hard work *worked*.

My big "aha" moment came when I realized my parents had passed their work ethic on to me. Not through direction but through osmosis. I learned there that you don't have to tell someone what to do, you must show them. Through my childhood, I learned hard work through their actions, not their words. To this day, it's a value I live by, and I continue to be inspired by it.

Another value I received was some words of wisdom from my father. In his younger years, my dad managed small finance companies. These companies loaned out small amounts of money to the average Joe. My dad was very successful at this. I remember going to my dad when I started my first company and asking him how to be a good manager. What he told me makes as much sense today as it did then.

"Take care of your people son, treat your employees right. You always do good in business if you do good for your people." I realized that along with hard work, this was yet another value I should live by. I would soon put that to the test.

2015 was one of the toughest years I've had in business. I was in my 5th year as a franchisee for a company called Liberty Tax. For reference, in 2009, I started with one franchise location. By 2013, I had 7 locations, and by 2015, I had 15 retail locations spread across a 100-mile radius. Talk about explosive growth. Back then, I thought I was a badass in the tax business. I literally thought no matter what I did, I couldn't fail. I talked with so much confidence that I had everyone believing me, even banks. That year I financed nearly $1,000,000 to support the growth. This was a big bet, doubling in size and hoping to score. When it was all said and done, on April 15th (the day tax season ended) I was still a million dollars in debt. I didn't know what to do.

The banks were calling, asking me to pay up. And I kept telling them I didn't have anything to pay them with.

This was the most uncomfortable situation I had ever been in. I didn't know what I was going to do. All I could think of was the fact that I was going to have to file for bankruptcy. All of these were such selfish thoughts. I remember walking into the office in late April and talking to my team about the results from the season. They couldn't believe how bad we had done, and neither could I. **Results don't lie**, is what comes to mind. As I explained to them what had happened, and how I was so uncertain of the future, I could see the fear in their eyes. They were scared to lose their jobs and I was scared to lose my business. As I spoke to them, I remembered my dad's advice: **"Take care of your people."**

As I left the office, I thought about them. I probably had about $60,000 in the bank. That may sound like a lot of money to most people, but I owed a *million dollars* to the bank, and they were breathing down my neck.

Usually, at the end of every tax season, I pay out a bonus to the employees. It's based on sales, but it's also based on results. We had a really bad year. Nobody on my team really excelled or did a particularly great job that year. Paying bonuses to people who didn't perform was something I had trouble doing, but I could hear my dad, and of course, myself, saying, "Even though these guys sucked (and I mean they really did) it was me. I was the one who sucked. I was the reason we failed, not them. Although they contributed, they weren't the main reason we failed. They weren't in charge and they did not make the decisions. The failure of the business was on me." With that in mind, **I had to make a decision between paying my employees or paying the bank.**

I knew both were the right things to do. Both were obligations I made and I knew I needed to commit to one. It was one of the toughest decisions I've ever had to make. The total bonuses were around $45,000. By paying them, I would be left with $15,000. Nowhere near the million dollars I owed. I took the weekend to make this decision and on Monday I called the bank.

This is what I told them, "I have a little bit of cash. I'm about to pay out bonuses, and when that's done, I'll send you what I can, but we're done. Y'all can have it all. The business is yours."

One of the toughest calls I have ever had. I was done!

Right after all this transpired, a few people called me and asked how I was doing, not knowing what I was going through. I told them, "You know what, I didn't do too well, as a matter of fact, I failed." One call was from a friend named Jerry. He just so happened to be somebody who had tried to mentor me for a long time. He had given me a lot of good advice, most of which I hadn't listened to.

I told him how bad I had done, although he already knew. He was in the same business as me and figured I was going through a tough time.

When he called, he told me he could help me through this. Even though I hadn't paid attention to his advice in the past, now his mentorship sounded appealing.

I agreed to take his advice and mentorship. He told me: "If you are committed, I can work with your bank and we can try to get you out of this mess."

"Thank you, but I don't know if this is something I can do," I replied.

"You know what, think about it. Send over all your financials. Let me look them over. Then, we can come up with a plan…."

So I gave him everything on a Friday. Over that weekend, he did some work, while I did some soul searching. On Monday, the call came in. It was Jerry.

"David, if I help you through this, but I want you to know that this is not going to be fun. In fact, it's going to be painful. You may not like me when I'm done, but we can get you out of this mess…."

Although it pained me to do this, I responded, "Okay, let's do it."

He began by promising the lender we'd be giving them weekly and monthly profit and loss reports. He promised we'd cut any and all expenses that were unnecessary or excessive. I literally had to downgrade the speed of my internet.

I didn't understand it then, but everything we did worked. It was amazing how efficient I got and how disciplined I became with my finances.

I remember committing to myself right then and there to never let this happen again. And it worked. I have now been able to put myself in a position to never ever let that happen again. Yet another value to live by.

I invested all my energy in getting better at reporting, putting financials together, and getting to a better place as a leader. So, in 2015, my big revelation was to say, "This will never happen to me again." More importantly, I learned I needed to invest more in myself because, at that point in time, I wasn't the person who could take our company to the next level. **I hadn't made the right investments in my knowledge, education, and skills to be able to control a multi-million-dollar company.**

The rule I took from this is that inaccurate numbers are junk.

Then, another revelation occurred. That was why we were *multimillionaires in debt.*

I share this story with you because, in 2015, I changed my whole life. Not only was I dating my wife-to-be, but I learned I needed to invest in myself. That year, I made the first large investment in myself… a personal development kind of investment. I went all-in, by joining a coaching and mentorship program with a guy named Tony Robbins (maybe you've heard of him?) I heard about Tony from a few friends who were very successful. They told me that Tony had changed their lives. I knew if they were seeing results that I should follow their advice, as I did with Jerry. To join the program with Tony was $20,000 plus a time and travel commitment. This was one of the largest investments I had ever made in myself and in my life. I remember signing the paperwork not knowing how I was going to do it. Did I have the money to do all this personal development? Well, not exactly… not at first. A lot of it came from me sacrificing a lot of pleasures in life, like eating out. I was willing to sacrifice doing those things so I could invest in myself. There was a lot of give and take. I had to finance this program through a finance company Tony partnered with. The interest rate was 17% so that meant I had to pay it off fast.

I realized at that point, there was no way I could do it alone. Going through that program, I read more than I've ever read before. I invested in planners and started to read and do courses at night.

The result was, in 2014, I didn't make very much money at all. Not in 2015 either. But you know what? In a year and a half, I was clear of that million dollars of debt.

I knew I never wanted to put myself in a position to lose that badly again. I wanted to be wealthy no matter the economy, even through a recession. If that sounds like more of my values and principles, it is!

Now, let's talk about you

You've heard some of my values and principles, I want you to start thinking about yours. As you begin to codify things, think about what your parents, grandparents, aunts, uncles, taught you through their words and actions. This is a great place to start, and you may be surprised by how much you've already learned from them, and how it's already affecting your beliefs. However, it's up to you to know if their values are in alignment with who you want to be and where you want to go.

I'm not here to tell you what's right or wrong as far as your values and principles, they're *yours* after all. But I'll tell you this: The way you know if something is right or wrong for you is by thinking about where you want to be, what you want to have, and how you want to be remembered.

If I were to look back at all the things I've done over my lifetime, I'm not happy about some of the things I've done. There are a lot of things I regret. But, even if I regret some things, they made me who I am today. It's my job now to understand that **whatever I do today makes me who I am tomorrow.**

Chances are, your current behaviors aren't totally in alignment with your values and principles. And, that's okay. Your economy may be out of whack. Think backward from how you want to be remembered, to today. Then let that guide you through your life.

Honor your values, and let your principles guide you.

CREATING YOUR RULES

Some people have rules for investing. They want to have 30% of their portfolio in a particular investment strategy, and 20% in another. They define rules that become a formula to determine how well they're doing. In losing weight, the rules tell you how many calories you can have. If you follow the rules, you will succeed at losing weight.

You've got to have the rules figured out before you can attempt to live by them. If you really want to be the person you wrote about in the previous chapter, the next step is to start actually living your life that way. The only way you can become the person you want to be is by having the right principles and values to guide you. There's no other way to do it.

Let's look at the components of your economy starting with your Values & Principles. As you go through each of the components, your rules will start to take shape. This will be the framework that will help you build your own economy.

VALUES & PRINCIPLES AKA RULES

Value and principles are what drive a person's decision making. You make decisions based on your principles and values every single day, even if you aren't aware of it. It's a subconscious compass that guides our actions. If you value health, you'll eat an apple, not a candy bar. But if you eat the candy bar, it's not because you don't value health, it's because you didn't use a decision-making tactic saying; does this pursue what I want in life or keep me from it? Is this attracting me toward the place I want to be, or pushing me further away? When you think of it in that way, you *will* put down the candy bar and pick up the apple.

When you start building your personal economy, you need to be sure of and be in touch with your values and principles. Don't feel like getting out of bed in the morning? Go back to your principles of productivity and personal health. Let your core beliefs guide your actions, and I guarantee you'll like the results.

HEALTH

Building an economy doesn't happen overnight. It's a long process that takes persistence and dedication, and even more than that, it takes time. You need to be sure before embarking on this process that you will have the vitality and stamina to continue this work for years to come, and that starts with your health.

Health is defined as your physical, mental, and social well-being. And your health can't wait! It determines what you're capable of doing, and therefore affects every other aspect of your economy. Health issues can be expensive, which then impacts your wealth, and thereby your legacy. These issues can be debilitating, forcing you to prioritize survival over success, thereby affecting your values and principles. If you're relying on doctors to keep you healthy, you're living in another economy besides your own. Having good health allows you the safety, security, and peace of mind you're striving for in building your personal economy.

WEALTH

Wealth is defined as an abundance of valuable possessions or money. Going further, I would say that when you have true wealth, you have excess. "Your cup runneth over." And the only way you can give to others is if you have an abundance or an excess. You can't give away what you don't have. Consider how much wealth you need to live securely and share your success with others. You can assess this with three simple questions.

- What type of wealth do you need to have in order to avoid any outside economic influence?
- Could you lose half of that and still be wealthy? **If not, it's not enough.**
- Do you have enough wealth to support generations to come?

In your economy, you're the boss. You cut the check. It's up to you to decide how much money you need. Once you've done that, I want you to double it. When you start to build your own economy you have to put yourself in the position to create wealth and abundance and refuse to settle for less. If you want the safety and security of a personal economy, it starts with the way you manage your money, and how much work you put in to get where you want to go.

Let's say you want to have enough wealth to support three generations. Keep in mind when considering wealth, you're building something not only for yourself but for those you leave behind. Do you have the kind of wealth that can be passed down to future generations? If not, you may need to rethink what wealth really means to you. Remember, you're not just creating wealth, you're building your legacy.

LEGACY

If you really want to leave a legacy behind, you have to define that legacy.

A good friend and mentor, Les Brown, once asked me a question that changed my perspective on the concept of a legacy. He asked,

"Do you know your great-great-great-grandfather's name?"

"No, I haven't got a clue."

"Well, do you know why you don't know his name?" He responded, "because he didn't leave you anything to remember him by."

Wow. His words really stayed with me. Without a legacy, he had nothing to be remembered by. Maybe my great-great-great-grandfather had a great personality, maybe he was a man of stature. I have no idea who he was. When I'm talking about a legacy, in this case, I'm not really talking about money, he could have been the president of a big bank, maybe he really stood up for a cause, or perhaps he built something tangible, like a building or a business. But my great-great-great-grandfather probably didn't do any of those things. If he had, we would know about it.

THE ONLY WAY THAT YOU WILL BE REMEMBERED IS BY WHAT YOU LEAVE BEHIND.

So are you going to leave an abundance of valuable possessions or money? In what way will you be remembered? If you build it right, and you build it strong, your personal economy will outlast you. You'll be able to pass it down and share it with future generations, and you'll be remembered for what you accomplished. If that's not motivation to get to work, I don't know what is.

Do you want to be remembered as a hard worker? A giver? A provider? Someone dedicated to service?

These components: Rules, Health, Wealth, and Legacy, are the core of your economy. When you begin the process of building your economy, these are where you have to start. Perhaps you're still scared to take that first step. Perhaps you still don't know where to start or understand why it's so important. If that's how you feel, I have a word of warning for you.

If you don't do it NOW, you may never do it. The toughest feeling to overcome is the feeling of REGRET. It's a horrible place to live. Don't hesitate or get paralyzed, write down your RULES NOW.

CHAPTER 6

BUILDING YOUR HEALTH

When my grandparents took me in, their parents, and even their grandparents were still alive. I was fortunate enough to get to see these wonderful people live out their lives. It taught me so much, in so many ways. I saw the love and affection that goes into taking care of elderly family members. I truly cherish those memories. However, it also brought me face to face with the reality of declining health and the effects of living an unhealthy life.

You see, I believe that elderly doesn't have to mean unhealthy, but if you don't value or control your health, you end up at the mercy of and dependent on others. And that's what I witnessed within my family.

As a young child, I remember watching my great-grandmother go through tremendous health challenges. She was diagnosed with high blood pressure, diabetes, and obesity. She did very little to address these issues, aside from the doctor-prescribed medications, so the burden of caring for her fell on my parents. They had to constantly check on her, and ensure that she was okay. That meant having to drive 2 hours to visit almost every weekend, where my parents would buy her groceries, home goods, pay her bills, and tend to her. We did this every weekend for years. There came a point when my parents just couldn't do it anymore, so they moved her closer to where we lived.

But her health only declined further. Her diabetes became more severe, and shortly after she was diagnosed with dementia. Over the course of two years, it ate away at her, destroying her faculties, making her entirely dependent on others. On top of the visits, grocery shopping, and bill paying, my mother was forced to sleep at her house almost every night. Her dementia made things incredibly difficult, and none of the health providers my parents attempted to employ stuck around for very long.

I watched my mom take care of her. Night after night, day after day. To add to this, my parents shared a car at the time and instead of being a burden to anyone early in the morning, my mother would get dropped off at night at my great-grandmother's home and then walk 2 miles home at 5 AM to get me ready for school and get ready for work. Finally, it became impossible to continue, and they were forced to put her into a nursing home. I knew that putting her in a nursing home wasn't a good idea, but the burden she placed on my parents had become too much for them to handle. She died a few months later in that nursing home, alone and probably afraid. Her dementia took a turn for the worst at the end, and she lost most of her cognitive thinking. Before her passing, she shared stories with me about things she was seeing on the TV, even though it hadn't been on, and of people who had come to visit her, but no one had come.

At the time, her passing was just the way things happened and life went on. I remember thinking it was just the way life was. I was sad to lose my great-grandma, but life goes on, right? Looking back, that was one of the many times I witnessed one person becoming dependent on another in my family.

My great-grandmother stole opportunities from my family. I didn't understand it at the time, but what I was watching was my great-grandmother, who chose not to take care of her health, slowly losing her independence. I also witnessed how much it cost my mother. Time, energy, and opportunity were taken from her. I'm not saying she shouldn't have loved or cared about my great-grandmother, but because she didn't take care of herself, she became dependent on our family. That dependency stole years from my mother. It took her time and her energy… which she could have invested in herself.

When my father was diagnosed with cancer, I watched him begin to slide into the same cycle. This time, cancer was the culprit, and the root issue was, once again, an unhealthy lifestyle. My mother was again faced with the task of caregiving. What my great-grandmother and my father hadn't understood is that they were not the sole sufferers. In fact, their poor health was stealing from someone else's life.

As I watched these progressions over the years, it made me value being healthy for the rest of my life. I realized I never want anyone to have to take care of me, not physically and not financially. It's not anyone else's problem. My health is my personal responsibility. I made a decision to not steal anyone else's time or energy to take care of me.

WHAT DOES GOOD HEALTH MEAN TO YOU?

In your economy, you get to decide what being healthy means. Everyone's definition is going to be different, and that's okay! I want you to define it clearly and specifically.

Having good health can mean not being dependent on medication or drugs to get through the day. Maybe good health to you is having enough energy to play with your children and not get winded. Good health must have both a nutritional, physical, and emotional gauge. You get to determine how much of each you need. I recommend you focus on all three and not one alone. They work together and are all required.

THAT TIME IN MEXICO

If we haven't met before, I would like to fancy myself as somewhat athletic, by no means an athlete, just simply athletic. So when I perform any physical activity, I'm pretty fast. I pride myself on being able to run, jump and be very active.

Let me add before I get to the story, I live in deep, deep, deep, did I say deep, South Texas. Where I live, we border Mexico. So quite often I have friends who travel down here to visit and we cross over to Mexico for the day to do tourist stuff.

On one occasion, a buddy of mine came down to Mexico with me. As we were crossing, he asked, "Isn't it very dangerous out here if you aren't from the area?" I responded, "Not really, it's a tourist area, nothing bad goes on here." An hour later we were walking down the street and we heard a loud sound, similar to a gunshot off in the distance. He looked over at me and said, "I thought you said it wasn't dangerous here?" I replied, "Well, here's why I'm not scared." I pointed down to the bridge that connects us back to the U.S. and said, "You see that bridge?" He replied, "Yes." I asked, "How fast do you think you can make it to that bridge?" He said, "I dunno, pretty fast." I replied, "Do you think you'll get there before me?" He said, "No way!" I replied, "Well, that's why I'm not scared. They'll get you before they get me!"

The lesson here is that my commitment to my health allowed me to feel confident in situations that might test my endurance or strength. After that last statement to my buddy, he laughed and called me an A-hole!

YOU ARE RESPONSIBLE FOR EVERYTHING THAT HAPPENS TO YOU. NOBODY ELSE!

BUILDING YOUR OWN ECONOMY

You are responsible for taking care of yourself. Nobody else. Ultimately, you're the only one you can rely on. If you're not taking care of yourself, there's a problem. Good health isn't about you. It's about everyone around you. Valuing good health is about the people who care about and love you because you care about and love them. You're showing them respect by taking care of yourself. You're able to deliver for them and give to them. You're able to contribute to the world. You're able to provide energy, support, and a successful livelihood, all through your practice of good health. The healthier you are, the more you can give to the world, the more energy you have, and the more opportunities you'll be afforded. So, when you take care of yourself, you're also taking care of the people around you.

THE MORE YOU TAKE CARE OF YOURSELF, THE MORE YOU'RE ACTUALLY TAKING CARE OF OTHERS.

In your personal economy, good health has to be a priority. Without good health, you will eventually become dependent on others. This puts you at the whim of doctors, surgeons, drug companies, and those you love. What's more important, you begin to affect the economies of your loved ones, who must expend emotional, mental, and even physical energy to help you do the things you should be able to do yourself. Just like my great-grandmother relied on my mom.

MY THOUGHTS ON MEDICATION.

    Personally, I'm not a strong believer in medication. While I take it when necessary, I choose instead, to do things like eat well, work out, and meditate. When at all possible, I say you should treat the root cause, not the symptom. Educate yourself on the ways to best care for your body, and put them into action sooner rather than later.

    It takes persistence and consistency, but caring for yourself in this way will allow you the freedom to live independently, and spare others the burden of your dependence. **Your health is the most valuable asset you can possess because, without it, you have nothing.**

    Your health is your responsibility, and it can't wait. Part of building your economy is doing your research and taking appropriate action to care for and maintain your health. Start now. Start today. There's not any time to waste.

One last example.
    I watched a video of one of the richest guys in the world, Warren Buffett. In this video, he was speaking to a young group of high school children. One of the kids asked him what his thoughts were on health. He responded by asking a question to the children.

    "Before I answer, I want you to think about a car. Not just any car, your dream car. What if you shared your dream car with me and I could gift it to you. Would you take it? All the children screamed, YES! Great, he stated. Before I gift you this car I need to let you know that if you accept this car, you have to follow a few rules.

"Here are the rules.
- You have to drive this car for the rest of your life.
- You cannot purchase another car/vehicle ever again.
- This car must last you your lifetime.
- You cannot trade it or sell it."

"Would you still take the car?"

Everyone had a confused face.

He then said, "Okay, let's say you said yes to the car. Now think about this, how well would you take care of the car, knowing that rules? Give me some examples of how you would care for it."

The kids shouted, wash it daily, maintenance, try not to abuse it, wax it, not eat in it, and so on.

Warren went on to say, "WOW that's good advice. Now I want you to think about that car as being your body. Your body, just like the gifted car, is the only one you'll ever get. You only get one and you have to take care of it all your life. How well should you take care of it?"

This story was so impactful for the children but even more impactful for me. We only get one body, your body is where your HEALTH lives. Being healthy is a lifelong decision and responsibility.

Here are some examples of Health Rules I live by and I challenge you to design your own.

RULES TO LIVE BY:

- Drink half of your body weight in ounces of water each day.
- Each plate of food should be composed of 50% fruits or vegetables.
- Set a target of 10,000 steps daily.
- Avoid fried and/or processed foods.
- Strength training burns more calories and fat than cardio.
- Investing in my health is more important than wealth.
- Health is more than just physical, it's mental.

CHAPTER 7

BUILDING YOUR WEALTH

To me, wealth means having an abundance of something valuable. It's the overflowing of possessions. **In order to build your own economy, you must have a foundation and a belief in wealth.** The challenge with that is, many people go through life not really understanding what wealth is. Most people believe that wealth means having a lot of money, but there's more to it. Each person has a different view about what "a lot of money" means, and it often depends on how many people you've been around who have money. That alone can determine what you believe wealth is. Your definition can also change over your lifetime.

My perception of wealth and my definition of being wealthy has changed a lot over the years. My parents purchased a modest home, a fixer-upper, for around $30,000 in 1985 when I was 2 years old. At that time, that was a lot of money. They spent almost every weekend for twenty years fixing that house. They believed in homeownership and this was part of their legacy to their children. I watched how they lovingly cared for their home, and I saw how they slowly, painstakingly made it into a place they loved.

Growing up, my parents told me "this home will be yours one day, mijo," which means son in Spanish. When I heard those words, I was ecstatic. I knew what it meant to them, and I was in awe that it would be mine someday. This meant I would always have a place to live. You see, in my teens, everyone is supposed to figure out what they are going to pursue in life. I, on the other hand, didn't have much of a clue. I had no idea what I was going to do to make money in life, and I surely didn't believe I would ever be able to own a home of my own. That was wealth to me.

Looking back, I can see how much my concept of wealth has changed since then. At that point, being wealthy and owning a home were synonymous to me. Today, I've surpassed every career and financial goal I could have dreamed of back then.

THE DAY IT ALL MADE SENSE

In late 2008, I sat in a room filled with 50 plus people all seeking to learn more about getting into the tax industry. I was there, not by choice, but by chance. I was kind of dragged to this event by a good friend and business partner, Kal. He asked me to join him at this event because he thought this was a great business opportunity for us to join.

I didn't have the same feelings about it that he did, but I respected him and attended anyway. To be very honest, I partially attended because it involved traveling and having a few nights out away from home. At this point in my life, I hadn't been exposed to much travel.

As I sat passively listening to the sales pitch, I kept hearing "recession-proof business" repeated over and over by each presenter. This really resonated with me because I had just gone through a recession that killed my real estate career. "Everyone needs to file a tax return, recession or not," the speakers said. They got my attention. From there forward, I listened attentively to the opportunity to join Liberty Tax. Each speaker made me think more and more about the opportunity. Toward the end of the day, they brought up some presenters that were franchisees, people who were doing what I was there to learn how to do. Each of them came up and shared their story. Where they started out in life, how they found Liberty Tax, what they were doing now, and most importantly, why we should join them.

I knew this was a sales tactic, but as I listened, I kept hearing subliminally, "A better quality of life is through this opportunity." Many of them had troubling pasts and no experience in the business, just like me, yet now, they had so much more going on in their lives. With every story shared, I couldn't help but want to be one of them. They were enjoying life, providing for their families, giving other people opportunities, and they all seemed so happy. I wanted to be like them!

Before the event, I thought I was doing okay. You don't know what's out there until you get around different people and things. These guys were making hundreds of thousands of dollars, some millions, and I was thinking making $40,000 was enough. Money aside, they had beautiful families, awesome lifestyles, and you could see the smiles across their faces were not forced. That day, I decided that I couldn't settle anymore for a lifestyle of just enough. I knew if I wanted to be like them I needed to work for an abundance. This meant I had to commit to my wealth.

WHAT DOES BEING WEALTHY MEAN TO YOU?

In your economy, you get to decide what being wealthy means. Everyone's definition is going to be different, and that's okay! I want you to define it clearly and specifically.

Remember, having wealth isn't just about having flashy cars or fancy clothes. Having wealth also gives you security and independence. If you truly want to exist within your own personal economy, you can't rely on other people or the government for financial support.

What type of wealth do you want to have? That's the most important question to ask yourself, and your unique answer will inform your decisions moving forward. Many people significantly underestimate what they're capable of producing. When I was young, I used to think that making $40,000 a year was a lot of money. I realize that might be a lot of money for you, I'm not trying to tell you that it's not. I am trying to say that if you make $40,000 a year, and you have one bad financial month where you get so sick you can't work, or your water heater breaks, or your refrigerator breaks, you're screwed. So many people are just one paycheck away from real trouble. They worry about what would happen if their car breaks down, or they get a flat tire. So many resign themselves to the idea of working forever because they're convinced what they have is all that can be had. When you're living like this, if even one of these things happens it would significantly impact your life. You also don't really have wealth in this situation.

WEALTH WITHOUT MONEY

To be super clear and straightforward, I know some readers will get to this section and offer their opinion on wealth. Many may agree with me but some will try and argue that wealth is not money, it's love, relationships, family, and so on. I agree with that to some degree, however, without money you can't support any of those. Money gives options to the other wealthy areas of your life. You can't provide for people if you are struggling. Get your money right so that you can give 10 times the love and support to those you care about.

QUICK ASSESSMENT

- What does wealth look like to you?
- How much wealth in $ do you need to have to leave generational wealth?

WHAT KIND OF WEALTH WOULD YOU NEED TO HAVE IN ORDER TO AVOID ANY OUTSIDE INFLUENCES ON YOUR WEALTH?

A good indicator of what wealth *should* look like is this. Think about the amount of money you previously identified as "wealth." If you lost half of it, would you still see yourself as wealthy? *That's real wealth.* Jeff Bezos, Elon Musk, and Bill Gates are some of the top income earners in the world. If any of them lost $20 billion in one day, they'd still be richer than anybody that's ever been alive. That's the kind of wealth we need to strive to have.

IS THERE ENOUGH?

I also think of wealth as the transfer of value *intergenerationally*. To be able to move wealth down the generational ladder is key, but very few people are in a position to do that. In my personal economy, that's what being wealthy means. It's an essential component.

HOW ARE YOU GOING TO GET THERE?

As you build your own economy, you need to have a wealth plan. Remember when I said wealth wasn't just about money? Well, your plan should go beyond just making money. Many people believe they're on the path to wealth but, often they haven't really thought about what wealth means to them.

WEALTH EQUALS FREEDOM.

You may not have been born with the benefit of generational wealth, but you can be the first in your familial line to begin passing it down. I'm living proof of that.

"IF YOU'RE BORN POOR, THAT ISN'T YOUR FAULT. IF YOU DIE POOR, THAT'S YOUR FAULT." – BILL GATES

FOOD FOR THOUGHT.

If you followed a wealthy person around all day and tracked the amount of energy and hours they spend on things that promote their wealth, how many hours do you think it would be?

Now ask yourself, do you believe they work more hours or expend more energy than the average person making $40,000 a year?

The answer is very easy to come up with. They spend the same amount of time as the rest of us. This gives hope to all of us seeking wealth. We all have the same amount of time. We all have the same 24 hours. That means we can all create wealth, all we have to do is use our time on activities that promote wealth.

ACTIVITIES THAT PROMOTE WEALTH

Imagine sitting down at a slot machine in Vegas. You insert a $20 bill and pull the lever. The wheel spins and you win $2. Now you have $22. Might not seem like much but you've just experienced a 10% gain on your money. That's a phenomenal return on investment. Before I continue, I don't want you to think that gambling is a form of wealth building but I want to continue to illustrate a point. What if you kept spinning the wheel and you kept winning $2 on every spin. No matter how many times you spun it, you won $2. How long would you sit there spinning the wheel? The answer I hope is that you'd never leave. The reality is, that you would have to leave eventually. This isn't building wealth, this is just working a job. You put in the time, and you get a return. What we are looking for are activities that don't require us to work.

The building of wealth is finding ways to get returns on your money without having to show up.

Find where you thrive and work tirelessly. Think big picture and long term. Make choices that will help bring you toward your personal definition of wealth, so you can enjoy the financial freedom of your own personal economy.

Now, let me ask again, *What does being wealthy mean to you?* Has it changed after reading this chapter? How much wealth do you really need? I'm not just talking about money, either. What about possessions? What about land? What about other assets? What other things can you leave behind? **That's true wealth.**

MY WEALTH BUILDING STRATEGY

The following chart breaks down my investment asset allocation. For a more in-depth breakdown and a worksheet, you can use, visit my website davidaperez.com/resources

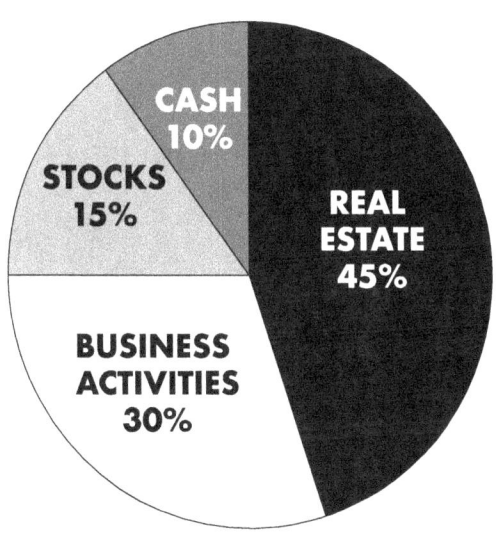

CHAPTER 8

BUILDING YOUR LEGACY

According to Webster's Dictionary, legacy is defined as something transmitted by or received from an ancestor or predecessor.

To better state this, I would like you to think of a legacy as a remembrance of you by the impact you created in the world.

Most people think of a legacy as money, property, or possessions. Those things are an important part of a legacy, but really, what we should be doing is striving to leave an impact that lasts generations. Your impact comes from the memories of you, and the values you instilled in others, and the things you left behind.

If you start today and live your life according to the strong values and principles you created in chapter 5, you can be certain that you are building a legacy.

BUILDING YOUR OWN ECONOMY

No matter which way you choose to live your life, you're going to leave a legacy. You'll be remembered by those who knew you in one way or another. The difference is, when you build your own economy, you actively, purposefully build a strong and powerful legacy. You get to dictate how you will be remembered. You pass on possessions and lessons that will carry your name.

There are a multitude of wonderful things we can leave behind. As unique as we all are, there are as many ways to be remembered as there are people. What we want to avoid, however, are the negative ways we can be remembered. We can probably all agree, these have no part in anyone's legacy. When you're building your economy, you want to avoid things like debt, negativity, or wrongdoings. I call these weeds. What we need to do is ensure we get rid of the weeds as soon as they start to take root.

IN THE GARDEN OF LIFE, YOU CAN EITHER PLANT FLOWERS OR GROW WEEDS.

In your economy, your legacy should be filled with flowers. "Flowers" are in the form of ideas, assets, values, impact, and influence. Whatever it may be for you, leave behind a garden full of flowers, and eliminate the weeds. And that's really what a legacy is all about. At the end of your life, either you planted a great garden, or you left behind a tangle of weeds.

FEEDING 5,000

In 2012, I started to make a little bit of money. It was the first time I'd ever seen money. I don't mean tons of money, just some profit. Until that point, everything I made went to pay bills and went back into the business. I felt compelled, with this newfound income, to give something back to the community that had supported me. I didn't know what to do or how to do it first but I knew that I had to do it. I hadn't been a giver most of my life, in fact, I believe I was more a taker. Something told me that year that it was now time to stop being a taker and start being a giver. It was late October 2012 when it hit me. The Thanksgiving holiday was fast approaching, which is one of my favorite holidays. Every year my family and I gathered for a meal, shared stories, and created memories that would last a lifetime. I always looked forward to our gathering. I recall one night closing up my office and one of my team members was with me. I asked, "Are you ready for Thanksgiving?" She replied in a very low voice, "I am." I asked what was the matter. She said that she was stressed because one of her kids lost their job and another was going through some tough times. She shared that she didn't know if they were going to come over to her house or if they could even have a Thanksgiving Dinner because of their hardships. It was then that I realized how fortunate I was. I had never thought that someone didn't have the same experience during Thanksgiving that I always did. So that was it, I decided to help families in need for Thanksgiving.

At first, it was all about food for me. I found families in need and delivered turkeys with all the trimmings to them. The first year I bought Thanksgiving Meals for ten families, and the next year it was twenty, and the year after that it was forty! I invited my team to join me to deliver each year. It was so much fun. The smiles and gratitude that you received were worth all the work.

In 2015, I decided that it was time to step it up. I wanted to feed 500 families. This was a HUGE jump for me. As I started to think, I realized that this could be bigger than me. I even started to realize what it was that I was actually doing. You see, I thought it was all about food. Although the food was part of it, the real giving was coming by way of memories. The meals brought families together which created memories. That became the message! Now it was time to get more people involved.

I made flyers, posted on social media, and rallied the community, trying to inspire others to give back as well. And, they did!

One of the greatest feelings is having my family and loved ones join in on the mission to feed families.

Now it's become an annual affair with many volunteers who participate to feed many families. That small effort in 2012 blossomed from my desire to help anywhere I could, and it turned into a nonprofit we named, **Free Hunger Nation**. It involves community-wide outreach and touches hundreds of people's lives each year. I also work hard to involve the children of both the volunteers and those receiving assistance. I want to instill the value of service in them and remind them there are good people in the world who are always there to lend a helping hand.

I don't tell this story to brag or laud my good deeds, but simply to illustrate the point that when you *can* make an impact, you should. I had no idea what that one small act of service would blossom into. I just wanted to do good and help my community. In the process, I am building a legacy I can truly be proud of, and it proves that a legacy isn't just something that happens once you're gone.

If you would like to join in and host a local event like the one we started, go to our website and request more info.

We can help you get this set up wherever you live.
www.freehungernation.com

A LEGACY IS SOMETHING THAT CAN CARRY YOUR REMEMBRANCE.

When we're young, we absorb values, ideas, and concepts from the people around us. If we're around successful people, the possibility of our own success seems certain. You may say, "I'm going to be a doctor, just like my dad." It's also possible to pass down limitations and doubt. If you come from a lower-income household (like me) it can be more difficult to picture yourself doing anything except what your parents did. You may actually hear well-meaning family members say, "We aren't rich people. Nobody in our family will ever go to college." It can be disheartening to hear. To realize that no one will *ever* leave you a garden can be very discouraging. But you can start planting your own today and be the first of many generations to sow seeds and tend a garden.

We're all born poor. We're all born afraid. We're all born naked. But, you all have to start somewhere. Somebody, at some point, has to decide to make their way and build a legacy. No matter where you come from, no matter what you've been through, all it takes is a decision to start. And that could be you today, right now. You can decide to be the one in your generation who will start! You can be the one to say, "This is us. This is what we do. This is who we are."

YOU HAVE TO INVEST YOUR TIME IN CREATING A LEGACY THAT'S WORTH REMEMBERING.

Values and principles are a huge part of a legacy. Wealth is too. You certainly want to leave behind assets, property, and money rather than debt. And, in terms of your legacy's impact upon future generations, health is just as significant. Taking care of yourself and your health will lead to your children being healthier. Instilling healthy habits and lifestyles in younger generations will make a huge impact on their quality of life, and for generations to come. It's important to think about who is watching you.

You can pass on wealth, but if you simply hand your money off to someone else without first instilling your values and principles in them, you've left behind an incomplete legacy. If the person who inherits your money doesn't share your values and principles, that money is going to disappear and your legacy ends then and there. It's a fancy flower bed with no flowers. We shouldn't be looking just to leave money or possessions behind anyway, we should want to leave behind values that will then protect and grow that legacy for generations to come. Then you're leaving behind perpetual wealth.

SO, WHERE SHOULD YOU START?

1. Ask yourself how you want to be remembered. Describe it to yourself in detail, then work backward from there to where you are now. You're going to reverse-engineer your legacy.

2. Define the values and principles you want to live by and be remembered for by reviewing them. Codify them and reference them constantly.

3. Put them into practice. Follow your values and principles faithfully. Doing the right thing all the time is hard, but it will make a difference in your life and in the way you are remembered.

More than anything, to create a lasting legacy you must have the freedom of independence. You have to make the decision to be completely independent and rely on no one but yourself to build something that will stand the test of time. You have to build your own economy. Do this, and future generations will celebrate you. They'll celebrate what you created, they'll celebrate what you did, and it won't just be because you left behind money. It will be because you left a legacy of good, a legacy of integrity, and a legacy of giving back.

MY TIPS TO BUILDING A LEGACY

Think big! The only way to think big is to be exposed to big thinkers. Get around people who are thinking so big that it takes a few minutes for you to even comprehend what they are doing. Get around people who force you to THINK. This will inspire your creativity and thoughts that will translate into legacy building.

Live life based on the rules you set. Share those rules as often as possible with those around you. Make sure everyone knows what you stand for and your reasoning behind decisions.

Be a self-promoter. You can only be remembered if you are known. If no one knows who you are, you'll never leave a legacy.

CHAPTER 9

WE CAN'T BUILD ANYTHING WITHOUT FAITH

Although this is a defined component of an economy, I believe faith plays a vital role in life. I felt compelled to have a chapter on faith.

Faith is, by definition, the complete trust or confidence in someone or something. Having faith is important because, in the path to building your own economy, you have to have some form of faith. Having faith in a higher power is part of that, but first and foremost, you really must have faith in yourself. Building your own economy requires self-confidence, but most people are their biggest critics. If someone gives you a compliment on something you did, a common response is, "Oh no. It was nothing. It's not very good at all."

Negativity is our default response, and because of that, having faith in yourself can be incredibly difficult. I challenge you to start believing in yourself. It's vital. You *can* be the controller and the driver of your own vehicle. If you're building your own economy, that's what you should be in pursuit of.

I also believe the concept of faith comes together with God and a higher power. You must have faith that you were put here to do great things, not to be mediocre, not to be average, and not to be dependent on someone else. You must believe to your core that this is true. You were gifted with all the capabilities to make it happen on your own.

I BELIEVE OUR GIFT FROM GOD IS LIFE, AND HOW WE LIVE OUR LIVES IS OUR GIFT TO GOD.

People today are so dependent on each other, our parents, the government, even our friends, to solve our problems or prevent us from failing. Support is great, but it's not what we should rely on. It's great knowing the people I love have my back, but I don't want to turn to them to solve my problems. I just want them to be my support. I love knowing there are people there to help me, but I love knowing that I don't need them even more.

Please know building your own economy is not about saying, "Screw the world, I don't need you!" It's not about turning your back on anyone. But it is about independence.

When a baby bird is old enough, it must open its wings for the first time and take a leap of faith. From that moment on, that bird has only itself to rely on, but you know what else happens? It learns to fly. If you have faith in yourself to leap into your independence, you too can soar to new heights.

Children take a bit longer than birds to be independent but give them a few years and they become very independent and strong. If they're raised in an environment where they're allowed to be themselves, they will be independent. Sure, they're going to get into trouble, they're going to get hurt, and they'll get dirty, but they'll do it with confidence. Children are fearless. They'll do things normal adults would never dream of doing. Fear keeps us dependent, we don't want anything bad to happen. But a child says, "I'm going to conquer the world!"

When they're young, kids are filled with confidence, energy, and charisma. As adults, that's really how we should be living our lives, but we don't. Nobody is born to be a dependent, but eventually, we get worn down by life and scared to fail (again) so we look for safety by living by someone else's rules.

In building an economy, you can program your mind, but you have to acknowledge the way your mind has already been programmed. You're the only one who can control your mindset. If you were programmed from day one to trust the decisions of others more than your own, it's going to be hard to have faith in yourself. You have to believe in what you can be, and retool your mindset to match that.

BUILDING YOUR OWN ECONOMY

My whole life, everybody told me I was special and I wasn't going to amount to much. I was told I was always going to be dependent on others. And, I believed it. I thought that way until I finally realized, through trial and error, it was utterly false.

Not everyone gets to have an epiphany as I did. We all have something to overcome, however. We all have some sort of limitation placed on us by others. Many get stuck in who their family is or how much money they have. If a family lives in a lower-income household, it can be hard to break out of that. The only way anyone is ever going to break free is by taking a leap of faith and making the decision to be in control over their life.

The most beautiful part about living within your own economy is that no matter what comes at you, it doesn't really matter. It doesn't affect you at all. You can confidently rely on yourself to handle anything, but, and this is key, you must truly believe in yourself.

The more I understand the rules of my own economy, the more I understand how to control it. It makes me even more committed to the habits I want to profess. For example, I went to a conference recently, and I made the decision to live according to my values and principles. I chose not to drink alcohol in the evenings like everyone else was, even though I wanted to. I put up with a lot of jokes at my expense, but I let them know the conference was important to me. I realized this was not the time or the place for it. I became very focused, and it was vital to me to take everything I was learning very seriously. I was in control, and what others did around me had no effect on my behavior. As long as they got their jobs done, it was fine with me. I also began thinking about the legacy I wanted to leave. I didn't want people to remember me as that fun guy who got drunk every night and showed up hungover every morning.

I wanted to stand firm on my commitment to myself and my growth. I wanted to be remembered as the man who did what it took to win.

IN THE PATH TO BUILDING YOUR OWN ECONOMY, YOU HAVE TO HAVE SOME FORM OF FAITH.

Standing strong in your faith is an important place to start when building your personal economy. Faith is a powerful motivator, and one of the keys to success. When you start the process of building your personal economy ask yourself the following:

- How much connection to faith do you want in your economy?
- How close do you want to be to a higher power?
- How close or far away are you from that right now?

Faith is the complete trust or confidence in someone or something. It's a belief. A belief not only in a higher power but also in yourself. It's the belief that everything will work out for the best. Faith extends not only to a higher power but to yourself. You must have faith in yourself that you can achieve your goals and are capable enough to build something that will last.

TIPS ON FAITH

I am not an avid churchgoer. In fact, it is very seldom that I attend church. I do however find time to thank God for the many blessings He has bestowed upon me daily. I believe in myself as much as God does. He gave me life, now it's my duty to live it. Faith is a choice!

Faith is the absence of fear. Be so committed to your economy that fear has no room to live.

CHAPTER 10

WE'RE BETTER TOGETHER (BONUS)

If you've read the book to this point, I hope I've convinced you that building your own economy is truly the only way for you to experience independence and freedom in your life. I've shared with you the core concepts or components that really build this economy, and I realize that, inherently, it probably all sounds very selfish. I have told you that it's really all about you and that you need to take personal responsibility. Your decisions control your outcome. I truly believe that it is a huge part of your success or your failure. It's in your control.

I have come to realize, however, that it's not really worth building a personal economy if you don't have someone to share it with. I didn't really truly understand how good or bad I was until I met my wife, Karen. She played a big part in helping me understand what it means to build an economy without even knowing it. When I met Karen, I was a young entrepreneur, aspiring to do great things in the world. I had a business that was growing rapidly. Frankly, I was flying by the seat of my pants, and loving it. I had figured out that my health was important, but I wasn't really committed. I had some core values that I thought were the right ones, but I wasn't consistent. I thought my legacy was going to involve me building a huge business, and that would be the end of it.

Meeting Karen forced me to think about more than just me. I didn't understand this at the time, and there were many arguments because I thought it *was* always about me and my economy. I was truly a selfish person before I met my wife. I thought all this was something I had to do for myself. That I had to succeed for me, do stuff for me, and get up for me. While I know it's important to make these types of decisions for ourselves, that really changed when I met Karen. She showed me how important it is to experience my economy with someone else. To truly have somebody buy into the same vision and mission and to truly love someone so much that the economy you're building is for them. Although in the beginning, we didn't always see eye to eye, the process has really helped to shape the concepts in this book. She has been a driving force for me to think bigger and want to do more because I want to show her what's possible.

I want a life of opportunity, a life of options, and a life of abundance for our future family. I know that's what we're doing today in building our own economy. I've seen so many people go into relationships not really having true clarity on what they want, who they want to become, or how they want to raise a family. And I truly feel blessed today, at the age of 37, knowing that a lot of that stuff has become clear to me through the formation of our economy.

In late 2020, my wife and I decided it would be a great idea to do more personal development together. Personal development can mean so many things, and I believe the development of oneself can happen in any area of your economy... your wealth, your health, your legacy building, or even your principles and values. In our case, we wanted to develop together as a couple.

> **I BELIEVE YOU CAN'T GO VERY FAR ALONE, YOU MAY GO FAST, BUT YOU CAN'T GO FAR.**

For the last few years of our relationship. I knew we had some struggles connecting at a very deep level, especially as it related to each other's goals and ambitions. So we decided to attend an event, it was a couples retreat, put on by one of my coaches and mentors at the time, Coach Micheal Burt. We had never done anything together as a couple like this, and we had no clue what was going to come out of it. We just knew that we were going to be able to get together and would probably be forced to share things together, and that's what I wanted. We knew it would probably be one of the hardest things we could do, but we also knew we needed to do it. The event was held in Seaside, Florida and, when we got there, Coach Burt said, "This isn't counseling, and this isn't going to be me talking about some of your deep-seated challenges from childhood. This is an event where I want you to get clear with each other on your God-given gifts, your talents, your abilities, your ambitions, and really share in a way that can help foster growth and synergy for the future."

I was very committed to making this happen, and my wife was too. I believe things always happen at the right time and this was the right time for us. Over the course of three days, we had the opportunity to really dig deep into what kind of goals we needed to set as a couple. I believe we must have shared goals. We also got to break down our individual goals, because I also believe we have to have some individual goals. We shouldn't always have to go for the same things. We should have a family goal, and we should have individual goals. I wanted Karen to have hers and she wanted me to have mine. And in those three days, we went through some of the deep, deep things we really needed to discuss – parenting, children, finances, wealth, and health. Those were the things we needed to discuss, and every time we got into one of these subjects, it was a little uncomfortable. I knew it was the right thing to do.

I share this story with you because, after walking away from that event, I could have just said, "Well, that was great." We could have just taken a few things from it, and gone on with our lives. But I believe if you are committed to your own economy, you'll realize that once you learn something that can benefit you, you must implement it immediately. You must change because an economy is ever-changing. It's not something that's ever going to stay the same. You can't rely on yesterday's solutions, there's always going to be a new solution if things change.

After my wife and I left the event, we realized it had changed our lives. It wasn't because of anything Coach said or the other members of the group said, it was because we said what we needed to say to each other. It's the unspoken things we hadn't said for years. We shared the belief that we are better together. Since then, my wife and I have really, truly tried to work together as a team, instead of competing against each other for attention or for our individual goals. We constantly work together and push each other in ways that a partner should.

If you're in a relationship now, or in your future relationships, I hope you will include your partner in your economy because you're building one together whether you know it or not. This isn't something temporary, this isn't something you just talk about. What you're going to be building with your partner is something that the world can't shake because, when you work together, you both guys together will be unstoppable. Starting today, I encourage you to look at your partner in a different way.

Ask yourself:
- Are we a team?
- How can this economy that we are building and working on be unstoppable?
- Are we the right people to make that happen?

If you said no to any of these questions, it's time to step it up. It's time to become the team you need to be.

I'd encourage you to get around other couples who are doing big things. I'd encourage you to go to events like the retreat we went to because that's how and where the growth happens. For us, it's where an epiphany happened, and it's where people start connecting at a higher level.

Without the value systems we've put in place, we would be very hard-pressed to make good decisions for our future. In thinking about raising children, we now know they'll be very successful with those values. We feel confident in being able to inspire a legacy, good health habits, and know how to teach them how to manage money. Today, I feel very confident that we can do all those things because we've committed to building them together.

I truly encourage you to share your plan with your significant other. Don't fight it. I think it's important that you and the person you love the most have a plan. My wife is my sounding board, my partner, my cheerleader, and my ass-kicker. She truly is the one person in the world who gets me. There's no way that any of what I've created, this book, my lifestyle, my success, and my failures could have happened without her. I don't believe that I truly understood how important having somebody by my side is… until I met Karen.

RESOURCES

My wife and I are working on a cool workbook to help you start working together with your significant other in building your economy together.

Check out our website davidaperez.com/couples

CONCLUSION

THIS ISN'T THE END, IT'S ONLY THE BEGINNING!

If you're not living in your own economy, you'll surrender very quickly to the opinion of others, or to the world, mainly because you feel you have no choice. You hand over your independence and exist in someone else's economy.

Writing this book has made me start thinking consciously about things I already knew, but wasn't practicing consistently. The concepts in this book have been with me for years, and they're a synthesis of all the teachings, training, experiences (good and bad) that have affected my heart, my brain, my thoughts, and my mindset. Even though I had all my concepts figured out, writing this really made me gain clarity. Where before I was sharing my ideas in a random order, I had to come up with a logical sequence in a useful, digestible format. Now, I feel more confident than ever in explaining my concepts to even more people. I'm also more confident in practicing what I'm professing.

As I instill these habits in my mind, I'm ingraining them and now they're permanently a part of me. It's made me a better person, and I'm more clearly defined now. Everything I do in the future will be more clear because my principles and values are sound.

To be in control of your life is one of the most empowering feelings you'll ever have. It's so euphoric. I've never won the lottery, but I would imagine this feels a lot like that. The similarity has nothing to do with money. **Controlling your own economy is like you've won the lottery in every area of your life**. Think about it. How would it feel if you won the lottery in health and wealth, and built a legacy for generations to come? And, picking the right values and principles is where it all starts. Then, you just continue to be blessed because of it.

The last, and probably most difficult aspect of building your own economy is one I haven't fully mastered. It has to do with truly being free from the opinions of others. It's one thing when, as an individual, you choose to not care what others think. That's the goal. It's a different thing, and much harder, when you're a business owner. One of the challenges I face in business is being concerned about offending customers and colleagues with my opinions or decisions. It's very difficult, and some days I walk a fine line. I know for a fact this is holding me back from truly owning my own economy.

TRULY SUCCESSFUL PEOPLE HAVE REAL FREEDOM IN LIFE.

Those top, highly successful people (think Warren Buffett, Jeff Bezos, Donald Trump, or Elon Musk) don't hold back their opinions or decisions. They don't hold back from anything. It's not that they aren't offending people, some of them are controversial in the way they communicate.

My point here is that they've each gotten to a place in life where they stand behind whatever decisions they make, and they come to their decisions on their own. They have faith it's the right thing, despite what anybody else says. It just doesn't matter to them.

The goal for you and me isn't to be as wealthy as them, or to offend people, be controversial, or be in a position where our opinions can sway markets. The goal is to live a life, as an individual and a business owner, where the opinions of others don't sway our decisions. Personally, I want to get to a place where I don't have to succumb to what someone else is telling me to do. And, I want to get there in all aspects of my life. Getting to a place where I know everything is going to be alright, no matter what happens in the world or with other people.

That's the end goal in all of this. Freedom. That's why we define and work toward wealth. That's why we learn about and care for our health. That's why we review and live by our values and principles. That's why we build a legacy we want to be remembered by. That's why we have faith in ourselves. So we can be independent, confident, and free.

Ultimately, you can and will make the decisions that shape your life, so let them be your own, and let them be ones that align with who you want to be, what you want to achieve, and how you want to be remembered. It's not easy, but nothing worth having ever is.

A BIG THANKS

I want to thank everyone who has helped contribute to this book. Over the course of my lifetime, I've had the opportunity to connect and network with so many beautiful people, each of whom I've taken a piece of to help put together this book.

I want to personally thank my parents Jesus & Elvira Perez for raising me right. Not perfectly, but right. They instilled the values and principles that I live by today, not just through their words, but also through their actions. They are truly beautiful people with amazing hearts, and I hope to continue to spread and pass on the legacy they have left behind in me.

I want to thank my birth mother, Dorinda Martinez. She truly knew what was best for me. I know it wasn't easy for her to let my grandparents raise me but because of her belief in a better life for me, I am who I am today.

To all my amazing family. There is not enough room in the book to share with you how blessed I truly am for having such an amazing family. There are so many memories of times where you taught me lessons, exposed me to new things, and guided me in the right direction. Your love shaped me.

I want to thank some of my friends who have really had a true impact on my life.

I want to thank my first best friend, Jaime Cisneros, for showing me what true friendship is, and helping me know anything is possible with the right support. You always believed in me brotha, I love you.

Thanks to my other best friend, Richard Garza, for sparking my desire to do more than I ever thought I could do. Your words meant so much to me growing up. I wouldn't be on this journey without you! I love you man!

To my good friend and business partner Kal Bhakta. Your belief in me is what lit the fire under my ass to get moving. Thank you for allowing me to be part of your family. Without your investment in me, I wouldn't have had the opportunities today that I do. I am truly thankful for all you've done for me Kal. I love you man!

To one of my mentors, Jerry Bayless. You have instilled in me some major discipline and helped me see the world from a different perspective. I didn't realize how lost I was in business and in life until I met you. I really want to thank you for not giving up on me, and for constantly telling me what I needed to hear. You are truly a great friend and a mentor, and I thank you for all you've done for me.

To the countless others who have inspired me through life, I want to thank you for allowing me to learn from you. Your presence made an impact in my life.

To my wife, Karen. Because of you, I can proudly say I've become the man I know my father wanted me to be. You've pushed me and challenged me to become a better man. For you, for our future children, for our community, and for those we care about. You really have changed who I am, and without you, I'd be lost. You are truly an inspiration to many. You light up the world with your beauty, your spirit, and your passion for helping others. Thank you, love!

TAKEAWAYS

TAKEAWAYS

TAKEAWAYS

TAKEAWAYS

www.ingramcontent.com/pod-product-compliance
Lightning Source LLC
Chambersburg PA
CBHW060846220526
45466CB00003B/1259